Innovation and Teaching Technologies

Marta Peris-Ortiz • Fernando J. Garrigós-Simón
Ignacio Gil Pechuán
Editors

Innovation and Teaching Technologies

New Directions in Research,
Practice and Policy

Editors
Marta Peris-Ortiz
Departamento de Organización de Empresas
Universitat Politècnica de València
Valencia, Spain

Fernando J. Garrigós-Simón
Departamento de Organización de Empresas
Universitat Politècnica de València
Valencia, Spain

Ignacio Gil Pechuán
Departamento de Organización de Empresas
Universitat Politècnica de València
Valencia, Spain

ISBN 978-3-319-04824-6   ISBN 978-3-319-04825-3 (eBook)
DOI 10.1007/978-3-319-04825-3
Springer Cham Heidelberg New York Dordrecht London

Library of Congress Control Number: 2014934152

© Springer International Publishing Switzerland 2014
This work is subject to copyright. All rights are reserved by the Publisher, whether the whole or part of the material is concerned, specifically the rights of translation, reprinting, reuse of illustrations, recitation, broadcasting, reproduction on microfilms or in any other physical way, and transmission or information storage and retrieval, electronic adaptation, computer software, or by similar or dissimilar methodology now known or hereafter developed. Exempted from this legal reservation are brief excerpts in connection with reviews or scholarly analysis or material supplied specifically for the purpose of being entered and executed on a computer system, for exclusive use by the purchaser of the work. Duplication of this publication or parts thereof is permitted only under the provisions of the Copyright Law of the Publisher's location, in its current version, and permission for use must always be obtained from Springer. Permissions for use may be obtained through RightsLink at the Copyright Clearance Center. Violations are liable to prosecution under the respective Copyright Law.
The use of general descriptive names, registered names, trademarks, service marks, etc. in this publication does not imply, even in the absence of a specific statement, that such names are exempt from the relevant protective laws and regulations and therefore free for general use.
While the advice and information in this book are believed to be true and accurate at the date of publication, neither the authors nor the editors nor the publisher can accept any legal responsibility for any errors or omissions that may be made. The publisher makes no warranty, express or implied, with respect to the material contained herein.

Printed on acid-free paper

Springer is part of Springer Science+Business Media (www.springer.com)

Foreword

Teaching Innovation

First of all, I would like to thank everyone who has contributed to this publication. Thanks to their dedication as they have provided a valuable and informative guide on a subject that is extremely important for our institution.

Technological advances have led to a revolution in education, a revolution which has caused a great many changes not only in the way we learn but also in the way that teachers are able to teach their students. With this, we have also seen an important change in the way that education is perceived. We are now constantly researching and developing new teaching methodologies, which has radically changed the way in which teachers now approach teaching.

Gone are the days where teachers can rely solely on the "chalk and talk" methods of the past, they now have to evolve. In this book/publication, we can discover these new ways of thinking and methods so that they can be put into practice and enhance students learning experiences, as well as develop teaching skills across all subjects and levels and in all kinds of institutions. This, in turn, leads to a constant improvement in the quality of education.

Nowadays it is possible to obtain a degree or a master online; thanks to the development of new applications, but is there more to innovation in teaching than technological advances? Do we all learn in the same way?

This publication considers development in all aspects of teaching and learning, from technological advances to the development of moral and teamwork competencies to different types of activities that favour other types of learning such as practical activities.

Most importantly, thanks to the collaboration of our colleagues. You can now learn how to put these innovations in teaching into practice in all types of learning environments.

Valencia, Spain   Francisco José Mora Más

Contents

1 **MOOCs, the Flipped Classroom, and Khan Academy Practices: The Implications of Augmented Learning** 1
Adolfo Plasencia and Natalia Navas

2 **Lessons Learned Through Massive Open Online Courses** 11
Mónica López-Sieben, Marta Peris-Ortiz, and Jaime Alonso Gómez

3 **Integration of Virtual Teaching/Learning Environments in Higher Education for the Development of Formative Assessment in the Field of Accounting** 23
Adelaida Ciudad-Gómez, Jesús Valverde-Berrocoso, and José Luis Coca-Pérez

4 **Developing Moral Competence in Higher Education** 31
Manuel Guillén, Michael O'Mara Shimek, and Ernesto de los Reyes

5 **Applying Concept Mapping: A New Learning Strategy in Business Organisation Courses** 41
Marta Peris-Ortiz, Diana Benito-Osorio, and Carlos Rueda-Armengot

6 **Pedagogical Innovation in Higher Education: Teachers' Perceptions** 51
Cristina Mesquita, Rui Pedro Lopes, José Álvarez García, and María de la Cruz del Río Rama

7 **Concept Mapping to Improve Higher Education** 61
Ignacio Gil Pechuán, M. Pilar Conesa García, and Antonio Navarro-García

8	Students' Performance with the Introduction of the Bologna Process: An Approach Via Quantile Regression	75
	Ana Fernández-Sainz, Jose Domingo García-Merino, and Sara Urionabarrenetxea-Zabalandikoetxea	
9	Exploring the Use of an ICT-Based Tool for Assessing Competencies in Postgraduate Students	87
	Fariza Achcaoucaou, Santiago Forgas-Coll, and Ramon Palau-Saumell	
10	A Proposal for Using Lego Serious Play in Education	99
	Jose O. Montesa-Andres, Fernando J. Garrigós-Simón, and Yeamduan Narangajavana	
11	Applying Teamwork Competence in a Company Course	109
	Teresa Barbera Ribera, Marta Palmer Gato, José Miguel Albarracín Guillem, and Carlos M. Dema Pérez	
12	*Co-creation Innovation* Model for Masters Programs in the Universities	117
	Gabriela Ribes-Giner, Agustin Peralt Rillo, and Ismael Moya Clemente	
13	Wearable Computers and Big Data: Interaction Paradigms for Knowledge Building in Higher Education	127
	Roberto Llorente and Maria Morant	
14	Designing Practical Activities for Skills Development	139
	Sofia Estelles-Miguel, Gregorio Rius-Sorolla, and Mario Gil	

Index 149

Contributors

Fariza Achcaoucaou Departament d'Economia i Organització d'Empreses, Facultat d'Economia i Empresa, Universitat de Barcelona, Barcelona, Spain

José Miguel Albarracín Guillem Departamento de Organización de Empresas, Universitat Politècnica de València, Valencia, Spain

José Álvarez García Departamento de Finanzas y Contabilidad, University of Extremadura, Cáceres, Spain

Teresa Barbera Ribera Departamento de Organización de Empresas, Universitat Politècnica de València, Valencia, Spain

Diana Benito-Osorio Departamento de Economía de la Empresa (Administración, Dirección y Organización), Rey Juan Carlos University, Madrid, Spain

Adelaida Ciudad-Gómez Accounting and Financial Economy Department, University of Extremadura, Cáceres, Spain

Ismael Moya Clemente Rectorado, Universidad Politécnica de Valencia, Valencia, Spain

José Luis Coca-Pérez Accounting and Financial Economy Department, University of Extremadura, Cáceres, Spain

M. Pilar Conesa García Departamento de Organización de Empresas, Universitat Politècnica de València, Valencia, Spain

María de la Cruz del Río Rama Departamento de Organización de Empresas y Márketing, University of Vigo, Vigo, Spain

Carlos M. Dema Pérez Departamento de Organización de Empresas, Universitat Politècnica de València, Valencia, Spain

Sofia Estelles-Miguel Departamento de Organización de Empresas, Universitat Politècnica de València, Valencia, Spain

Ana Fernández-Sainz Facultad de Cc. Económicas y Empresariales, Departamento Economía Aplicada III (Econometría y Estadística), Universidad del País Vasco/Euskal Herriko Unibertsitatea, Bilbao, Spain

Santiago Forgas-Coll Departament d'Economia i Organització d'Empreses, Facultat d'Economia i Empresa, Universitat de Barcelona, Barcelona, Spain

Jose Domingo García-Merino Facultad de Cc. Económicas y Empresariales, Departamento Economía Financiera II (Economía de la Empresa y Comercialización), Universidad del País Vasco/Euskal Herriko, Bilbao, Spain

Fernando J. Garrigós-Simón Departamento de Organización de Empresas, Universitat Politècnica de València, Valencia, Spain

Marta Palmer Gato Departamento de Organización de Empresas, Universitat Politècnica de València, Valencia, Spain

Mario Gil C.M.Mendaur, Universidad de Navarra, Pamplona, Navarra, Spain

Ignacio Gil Pechuán Departamento de Organización de Empresas, Universitat Politècnica de València, Valencia, Spain

Jaime Alonso Gómez University of San Diego, School of Business, Alcalá Park-Coronado, San Diego, CA, USA

Manuel Guillén Management Department & IECO-UNESCO Chair (UV-UPV), University of Valencia School of Economics, Valencia, Spain

Roberto Llorente Departamento de Comunicaciones, Universitat Politècnica de València, Valencia, Spain

Rui Pedro Lopes Department of Informatics and Communications, Polytechnic Institute of Bragança, Bragança, Portugal

Mónica López-Sieben Centro de Formación Permanente, Universitat Politècnica de València, Valencia, Spain

Cristina Mesquita Department of Social Sciences, Polytechnic Institute of Bragança, Bragança, Portugal

Jose O. Montesa-Andres Departamento de Organización de Empresas, Universitat Politècnica de València, Valencia, Spain

Maria Morant Centro de Tecnología Nanofónica, Universitat Politècnica de València, Valencia, Spain

Yeamduan Narangajavana Business School, Walailak University, Thasala District, Thailand

Antonio Navarro-García Facultad de CC. Economicas y Empresariales, Departamento de Organización de Empresas y Márketing, Universidad de Sevilla, Valencia, Spain

Natalia Navas Department of Audiovisual Communication, Universidad Nacional de Educación a Distancia (UNED), Valencia, Spain

Michael O'Mara Shimek School of Education and Sports, Catholic University of Valencia, Valencia, Spain

Ramon Palau-Saumell Institut Quimic de Sarrià, IQS School of Management, Universitat Ramon Liull, Barcelona, Spain

Marta Peris-Ortiz Departamento de Organización de Empresas, Universitat Politècnica de València, Valencia, Spain

Adolfo Plasencia Máster Comunicación y Educación en la Red. UNED, Valencia, Spain

Ernesto de los Reyes Institute of Innovation and Knowledge Management INGENIO (CSIC-UPV), Polytechnic University of Valencia, Valencia, Spain

Gabriela Ribes-Giner Departamento de Organización de Empresas, Universidad Politécnica de Valencia, Valencia, Spain

Agustin Peralt Rillo Departamento de Organización de Empresas, Universidad Politécnica de Valencia, Valencia, Spain

Gregorio Rius-Sorolla Departamento de Organización de Empresas, Universitat Politècnica de València, Valencia, Spain

Carlos Rueda-Armengot Departamento de Organización de Empresas, Universitat Politècnica de València, Valencia, Spain

Sara Urionabarrenetxea-Zabalandikoetxea Facultad de Cc. Económicas y Empresariales, Departamento Economía Financiera II (Economía de la Empresa y Comercialización), Universidad del País Vasco/Euskal Herriko Unibertsitatea, Bilbao, Spain

Jesús Valverde-Berrocoso Department of Education, University of Extremadura, Cáceres, Spain

Chapter 1
MOOCs, the Flipped Classroom, and Khan Academy Practices: The Implications of Augmented Learning

Adolfo Plasencia and Natalia Navas

Abstract Learning paradigms and practices are currently undergoing enormous transformations. Online learning is a reconfiguration of pre-Internet approaches. Peer-to-peer, non-hierarchical learning is made possible by the emergence of a mobile Internet that permits shared distance learning through "ubiquitous connectivity." Many universities and educational institutions around the world feverishly investigate and pursue the promises of new forms of technology-based online learning. Heralded examples are Massive Open Online Courses, the "Flipped Classroom" (also called the "Post-Lecture Classroom," the "Condensed Classroom," and even the "Hybrid Classroom"); and the methods employed by the Khan Academy (form-based learning incorporating a digital audiovisual tutorial mode and initially free online access). These new learning models do not replace their traditional counterparts but rather recombine them in a hybrid pattern we propose here to call "augmented learning" that includes significant components of informal as well as horizontal and self-organized learning.

1.1 Introduction

Do not be afraid to do things they never taught you to do

Steve Wozniak

Cyberspace, according to Pierre Lévy, is an interactive and collective communication method, which is different from the traditional ones we had known until now.

A. Plasencia (✉)
Máster Comunicación y Educación en la Red. UNED,
Almirante Cadarso, 46005 Valencia, Spain
e-mail: adolfoplasencia@gmail.com

N. Navas
Audiovisual Communication Department, Universidad Nacional de Educación
a Distancia (UNED), Almirante Cadarso, 46005 Valencia, Spain
e-mail: natalianavasgonzalez@gmail.com

M. Peris-Ortiz et al. (eds.), *Innovation and Teaching Technologies: New Directions in Research, Practice and Policy*, DOI 10.1007/978-3-319-04825-3_1,
© Springer International Publishing Switzerland 2014

It promotes a one-way mass media communication, in the same way as newspapers, the radio, and TV. On that part of cyberspace which is the Internet, communication goes both ways right from the beginning. Everybody is EMEREC (*Emetteur-Recepteur*) (Cloutier 1992) and is an active and integral part of the communication process. Lévy explains (Cloutier 1992) "three are the principles that have guided initial growth of cyberspace: interconnection, virtual communities, and collective intelligence" (Lévy 2004). However, it was only with the creation of the World Wide Web (WWW) (W3C 1990) at CERN, by Tim Berners-Lee and Robert Cailleau in November 1990, based on a hypertext system (Wardrip-Fruin 2004); and with the announcement of the official statement from the CERN that the web would be free to all on April 3, 1993 (CERN 2003 April 30), when it began to widespread with exponential growth, and as a means of all-to-all communication, in contrast to *mass media* communication (Gerbner M./M. McLuhan). Today it is shared by 2,400 million users around the globe (Miniwatts Marketing Group 2012).

By 1970, early developments of Artificial Intelligence (AI) began to be known, supported by previous background such as the "Teaching Machine" of the behaviorist, psychologist, inventor, and social philosopher, B.F. Skinner, who proposed it to practice "Programmed Instruction." Such Programmed Instruction eventually generated huge expectations which led to frustrations when these were not met.

Present forms of learning based on digital technology and the Internet cannot be considered really new but rather belonging to a current wave of technological developments which is heir to the "adaptive learning" or "intelligent tutoring" statements that proposed the use of computers as interactive teaching devices as far back as the 1970s, due to the rocketing computer power leading to emerging capabilities.

Today, the giant Internet upheaval combined with the capabilities of mobile telephone services is leading to a new hype in forms of learning based on the rupture of space and time in the use of knowledge, now free from the hard copies. The companies, as well as universities are a major player in that hype. Most pioneers are *Udacity*, founded by Sebastian Truhn—after leaving Stanford—together with David Stavens and Mike Sokolsky—in February 2011, and *Coursera*, founded by Andrew Ng and Daphne Koller in October 2011.

1.2 What Do We Mean by "Augmented Learning?"

We propose the term "Augmented Learning" to describe learning that "augments" or extends the traditional formal education, blending into it and using the new digital media, both computers and digital devices to this aim, with ubiquitous connection tools that offer different possibilities based on the Internet Social Media.

Practices and learning outcomes obtained with the above ubiquitous connection means and not tied to a physical location or a formalized schedule could also be called "connected learning," its main constraint being the possibility of access to interaction and content in digital format and distributed in the cloud (Cloud Computing). The access takes place via the Internet through a broadband connection having sufficient bandwidth. Therefore, it can be said that it can occur "any time, any place."

We understand the meaning of this term in the sense of the work published by Douglas Engelbart in 1962, called *Augmenting Human Intellect: A Conceptual Framework* (Engelbart 1962), since it refers to "augment" the human intellect, and to the IQ increase as a result of "the joint evolution of the capabilities of the human species and the technology it can produce." Engelbart stated 50 years ago, "computer mediated communication may promote the emergence of new collaborative work environments" (Aguirre 2013), this mediated communication is starting to be used on a large-scale basis for both "connected learning" and collaborative learning.

We call it "augmented learning" since it can be combined or overlapped—this being an informal and ubiquitous learning—into formal learning, to complement it and thus increase learning resulting from formal, organized and physically located—i.e., traditional—education. In this respect, it would be, in effect, a "hybrid learning" in the same way as for instance, the new "Flipped Classroom," also called "Post-Lecture Classroom" or "Condensed Classroom" and even "Hybrid Classroom," also known with other denominations. The terminology is not yet stabilized.

This "augmented learning," which is the sum of formal and informal education, also requires a "skills and capacity building" by the individual practicing it, since he/she makes extensive use of digital technology both in terms of software, hardware, and Internet resources. These skills and capacity building belong to those that Henry Jenkins includes in the "New Media Literacy" which are described in the White Paper of his New Media Literacy Project (Clinton et al. 2006), detailed below. Furthermore, the "augmented learning" is not only an individual process as far as in its informal part, the individual makes use of his/her "connected" status to gather information and contents, and also uses that same connection for individual practices and dual and collective social "peer to peer" interaction with "colleagues" or "peers," i.e., in a non-hierarchical, horizontal mode. This relationship and collaboration is very important, for instance, in the educational activities of the "MOOCs" (Massive Open Online Courses), "Flipped Classroom" type, etc., and it has been enhanced with the Social Web tools allowing you to remotely share digital space or work interface, content or conversations, multi-interface mode, and even multiscreen mode. The Google+ interface with added windows for shared video calls and social media streams, etc., from computer and/or mobile devices, is one of many massive use examples.

1.3 The Magnitude and Contagion Power of Technological Changes in the Educational Model: Four Factors

The sum and convergence of technologies allows us to expand the Internet extensions throughout the infrastructure of the mobile telephone services. Even if, in principle, such infrastructure was created only for calls and synchronous voice connections, today we can connect to the Internet from anywhere we have mobile phone coverage. In addition, the highly evolved economic methods of telephony itself have turned ubiquitous telephone connection into an Internet flat rate—low-cost. This had very important social implications and thus, Internet access is now available to many people in poor areas of the planet, causing the typical development stages in the first world to be skipped, from the deployment of fixed public telephone networks based on cooper cable to—and this is surprising for us—the Internet connection via computer. As a result, people today in Africa who have never had a fixed phone or home computer connected to the Web, now connect to the Internet every day using their mobile phones. The implications for learning are tremendous, with all of its consequences. Just an illustrative example: the *Wikipedia Zero* project (Wikimedia Foundation 2013), is an initiative of the Wikimedia Foundation to allow mobile access to Wikipedia in developing countries, using simple mobile phones—not smartphones—which are the most common in Africa, although this is quickly changing.

The advent of the possibility of what we call "augmented learning" based on digital technology and the web has been the result of at least four concurrent factors:

Hardware evolution: the relentless advance of Moore's Law has enabled mobile phones to have chips as powerful in computing power as a computer while mobile infrastructure is extending bandwidth and data management on a large scale, with only a small part of it being used for voice services. The tablet has emerged as a paradigm of the Post-PC Era. In the words of Steve Jobs: "This transformation is going to make some people uneasy… because the PC has taken us a long ways. It's brilliant. We like to talk about the post-PC era, but when it really starts to happen, it's uncomfortable […] Is it the iPad? Who knows?" (Fried 2010).

Software evolution: The Web develops, thanks to a new family of W3C standards and, as Tim O'Reilly announced in 2004, this leads to a new "architecture of participation" (O'Reilly 2005). The second half of the first decade of the twenty-first century has shown an exponential, astonishing, and successful use of Web 2.0 as a Social Web, in many specific manifestations such as social network services, ranging from initial *Flickr*, to the successful *Facebook*, *Twitter*, *Tumblr*, or *WhatsApp* now used more extensively in mobile devices than in a computer connection. To get an idea of the scale, *The Faces of Facebook* project (Rojas 2013), by Natalia Rojas, showed that on September 29, 2013, the Facebook Social Network had over 1.200 million—1.267.191.915 exactly—active accounts and still growing.

The mobile Internet connection would not make sense without a new paradigm of specific purpose software (Doctorow), as opposed to "general purpose computing" (Dailymotion 2011). This paradigm is based on the Apps or micro-applications of lightweight software, which can fully utilize the technical performance potential of the small chips placed in connected mobile phones and other devices. This is a radically different type of software, dedicated to a specific purpose and characterized by a tiny learning curve. It belongs to a new economy: the "App Economy," whose dimension is staggering: users have already downloaded more than 100,000 millions of Apps over the network. Those are downloaded from virtual stores like App Store (Apple) (Apple Inc. 2013a), Google Play (Google 2013), etc. They are a great tool not only for leisure and social networks, but also for "augmented learning" (Apple Inc. 2013b). In this connection, it is also significant that Google has launched an educational version for Google Play (Mateos 2013). This was at first a leisure Apps store, but now you can find Apps in it to learn anything you want. A new and real "App learning" is gathering pace.

1. *Space–time rupture in educational dynamics*: The space–time rupture in educational dynamics has implications in the operation and coordination of the human intellectual ecosystem in terms of organization of the education as well as on how educational actions were historically performed (master classes within four walls). Changes in the immaterial sphere introduce new forms of logic not to replace the old ones but to combine with them, thus fairly increasing the previous complexity levels of the physical education world. The formal system of educational functioning is in no way prepared for this level of complexity and that causes a great deal of turbulence and conflict in the academic world. The traditional dichotomy of the physical world: inside/outside the classroom has been fractured by mobile technology and ubiquitous connection, not only for Internet access, but also to exchange and share valuable information for educational purposes.
2. *Articulating personal and social behavior of users*: well equipped with new technological tools the users, once outside the physical classroom, can turn any place outside into a classroom without walls. Until very recently what is happening today with ubiquitous connection and learning anywhere, had no such electronics and real-time dimension. Any student could take a book or a text, or materials belonging to his formal education to any place outside the classroom, but the dimension you can have access to, whenever you have a good broadband connection cannot be compared with the quantity of paper books and printed documents that one person can carry with him/her. As it is always the case with tool-induced changes, positive and negative consequences are associated to it. The positive ones are similar to those previously described. A new negative consequence is, for instance, that as it happens with ubiquitous connection tools (with devices but also interfaces and user applications), the same device is used for "learning" or working purposes and for leisure and entertainment. As a result, a critical and indispensable self-organization task is required, adding to new abilities, whose best description are the "eleven skills" (Jenkins et al. 2009) defined by Henry Jenkins, for the "emerging participatory culture," but which are perfectly suited to the "New Media Education" of the twenty-first century: "(1) *Play*: the capacity to experiment with your surroundings as a form of problem-solving; (2) *Performance*: the ability to adopt alternative identities for the purpose of improvisation and discovery; (3) *Simulation*: the ability to interpret and construct dynamic models of real-world processes; (4) *Appropriation*: the ability to meaningfully sample and remix media content; (5) *Multitasking*: the ability to scan one's environment and shift focus as needed to salient details; (6) *Distributed cognition*: the ability to interact meaningfully with tools that expand mental capacities; (7) *Collective intelligence*: the ability to pool knowledge and compare notes with others toward a common goal; (8) *Judgment*: the ability to evaluate the reliability and credibility of different information source;

(9) *Transmedia navigation*: the ability to follow the flow of stories and information across multiple modalities; (10) *Networking*: the ability to search for, synthesize, and disseminate information; (11) *Negotiation*: the ability to travel across diverse communities, discerning and respecting multiple perspectives, and grasping and following alternative norms."

Since our time is limited, being able to process, thousand or one million times more information than has traditionally been the case for learning purposes, demands new skills that not everybody has, making it easy to fall into "procrastination" (dedicate more time to trivial things than to essential tasks). Choosing the right hierarchy and priorities in what you are doing or you could do with the benefits technology is providing to you in a given time is becoming one of the main issues of present technology-mediated learning.

1.4 On the Subject of MOOCs, Flipped Classroom, and Khan Academy Practices

The term MOOCs was coined by Dave Cormier of University of Prince Edward Island when his open online course called *Connectivism and Connective Knowledge* (CCK08) got an enormous success and reached almost 2,300 students, then becoming a massive course. The MOOCs phenomenon has been globally most successful all of a sudden.

For a training or educational activity to be called MOOC: (a) it should be structured as a course that includes assessments to test the learning level of the knowledge taught; (b) it should be global and massive in nature and students should be able to participate without any geographical restrictions; (c) it should be taught online. In addition to the ordinary contents of conventional courses, such as videos, lectures, and problem-solving publications, MOOCs also integrate user's interactive fora, with the aim of building a community-integrating students, teachers, and teacher assistants (TAs), exchanging information with each other as part of the course. Obviously a teacher needs technological assistance in addition to a human team. Teachers use artificial intelligence-based cybernetics with the so-called *OnLine Advanced Learning Interactive Systems*. Cursera and Udacity are involved in delivering MOOCs using this type of powerful cybernetic bases.

Israel Ruiz, VP Executive Vice President and Treasurer of MIT who is involved in the economic model of *edX*, the MOOCs platform launched by his university in collaboration with Harvard University, stated in his speech at the EmTech Spain Conference, in November 2013, that edX "already has 2.5 million users from around the world, generating online content through MITx" (MIT Technology Review 2013). The MOOC edX courses have students aged between 14 and 74 years. These courses with no limits help the MIT to "identify the universities structure, the education will be much more comprehensive and 'online' and rigid semesters will be replaced with more flexible 'modules.'" Students from universities around the world have launched themselves upon this adventure. And a sign of this "success" is that in some universities, students enrolled in their MOOCs have already exceeded the total number of "in-classroom" students. If success continues at the present rate, which I think is not at all guaranteed, the role and position of universities in the world should largely be reconsidered. This could be one of the biggest and broadest social debates globally.

The case of the "Flipped Classroom" presented by Ian Bogost in his article entitled *The Condensed Classroom* (Bogost 2013) with a picture of a traditional class placed face down to illustrate the play on terms like "flip teaching" and many other names like "upside-down class," "inverted class," "hybrid class," and "post-lecture class." In essence, according to Pascal-Emmanuel, the "Flipped Classroom," model, includes the following actions: (a) Students follow video-classes using their computers or mobile devices at home; (b) teachers record and produce video-classes, instead of delivering their courses in the classroom; the teacher can use his class time to work one-to-one with those students requiring additional help; (c) Students spend their classroom time actively working instead of passively sit listening to the teacher, and additionally the nonlinear characteristics of the digital video allow students spending more time learning the most difficult issues and asynchronically "augment" their dedication to those issues. They can thus learn at their own pace; (d) the "flip teaching" model ensures that any student, regardless of his/her socio-economic background will get support at home; (e) with the help of software, the teacher can quickly diagnose the parts where the student is progressing and those in which is having difficulties; (f) having video contents available online allow students a flexible self-management of the learning process as far as the live teacher's audiovisual lecturing is ubiquitously accessible. The "Flipped Classroom" combines in-class teaching and online activities. A survey carried performed following this model by the company Echo 360° shows that while 75 % of the respondent students in 2012 said—before experiencing the "Flipped Classroom" that they preferred conventional courses, after having tried them almost 90 % answered that they preferred "flip teaching." Nevertheless, the first course in which the model was introduced performance increased between a 2.5 and a 2.6 % and the second year rose by 5.1 % (Echo 360 2013).

The Khan Academy classes in audiovisual and online mode, edited and created using highly sophisticated electronic media in audiovisual formats are considered a success in learning processes using the new digital tools. Many of the Khan videos have been downloaded from the network tens of millions of times. In fact, Khan Academy courses are based on digital video. The Khan Academy is a nonprofit educational organization based on a web platform created in 2006 by American educator Salman Khan, a graduate of MIT and Harvard University. According to Khan, his mission is to "provide a high quality education to anyone, anywhere." His users have already downloaded from the Web over 235 million "lessons" (classes). His success is undeniable. It is a fact that these new learning forms are going to transform universities, but we think that web-based learning and education is not going to replace but rather transform education, as Ruiz puts it, and adds an "incremental" factor to traditional learning and to the combination of what is usually learnt outside (in terms of time and space) and inside. This resulting "learning Mix" is what we call "augmented learning." The result of it is greater than the sum of its parts. We are sure of it.

1.5 Conclusion

This new combinatorics of augmented learning is really new and we do not have yet enough experience to analyze the scope of the transformation that this is going to cause in the learning modes we used to know as far as this phenomenon is just beginning but the speed of technological change shows exponential growth rates in the appropriation of technologies and the *Social Media*, also due to its ease of use. We believe that its transforming capacity is huge as far as these are substantial changes for the educational world which is why is going to force the educational world to start a thorough rethinking of the educational organization at all levels both hierarchical and practical. Examples of this great success are already mentioned in the title: MOOCs; the "Flipped Classroom" also known as the "Post-Lecture Classroom" or "Condensed Classroom," which are learning proposals based on the free, digital, audiovisual tutorial with online access.

Technological applications themselves are changing as they come from new, still emerging, technological combinations. Even its semantics is changing as far as the new terms for the new technological practices and the new learning forms based on them, as well as the supporting technologies are in full upswing and linked to a trial-and-error development process. Very recent opinions from Sebastian Thrun, who pioneered the MOOCs at the Stanford University and now with his company Udacity perfectly illustrate the case (Chafkin 2013). Anyway, with this important caveat, the new learning forms that we are mentioning here, which would be impossible without the contribution of digital technologies, mainly those of the digital video and its postproduction as well as the creation of distributed contents (creation, storage, access provision, Cloud computing) through the Internet. The early adopters of these types of tools have shown the educational community the most innovative way to "hack" such tools, which were originally thought for leisure and entertainment digital business in the Social Media, in order to generate new uses in education and learning (Plasencia 2013). Through these forms of teaching, in a bottom-up process and learning from this de-hierarchization, the most advanced universities are the leaders of this experimental process to use those tools on a large scale, creating ad hoc platforms.

The MIT launched a pioneering platform, MITx, to deliver MOOCs and renamed it as "edX," in collaboration with Harvard University. It was a joint launch in May 2012 and Berkeley joined them almost immediately. Subsequently dozens of universities in the USA and hundreds of educational institutions all over the world followed the same path in a list which is continuously increasing.

We believe that MOOCs and "flipped," "hybrid," or "condensed" classroom are parallel learning form, which are complementary to the conventional and formal learning. All these new learning forms have peer-to-peer learning elements and actually form a "hybrid learning" and an extension of formal learning producing in practice an "augmented learning" in people, hence the title of our chapter.

Perhaps in the near future, conventional learning forms will evolve toward current MOOCs, "Flipped Learning," or the proposals of the Khan Academy, Udacity, and the like, which still do not belong to formal learning, but today they form a set of new educational forms, including informal learning of technology base, and actually "augment" and complement traditional formal educational world practices in a hybrid of "Recombinant Media" a notion that William J. Mitchell used in a visionary mode, in the field of architecture and *New Media* linked to it, in his book *City of Bits* (Mitchell 1997). We understand such education and hybrid learning as an "augmented learning," in the Engelbart sense. Obviously, these practices are quite new and still experimental and there is very little scientific literature on the subject. For all those reasons, many sources of this work, in spite of being authors and publications of great prestige, not necessarily come from the orthodox spectrum of publications and scientific papers.

Acknowledgements We thank Douglas Morgenstern, Senior Lecturer, Emeritus at MIT and Extension Instructor at Harvard University, for his advice and invaluable assistance and help; Roberto Aparici, Profesor Titular en Comunicación y Educación at the Universidad Nacional de Educación a Distancia (UNED) and Director del Master de Comunicación y Educación en la Red, for his valuable lessons and assistance (UNED); Sara Osuna Acedo, Vicerrectora Adjunta de Formación Permanente y Secretaria Académica del Master de Comunicación y Educación en la Red (UNED), for her continued unconditional support; and Ignacio Gil Pechuán, Catedrático de Escuela Universitaria at the Departamento de Organización de Empresas at Universidad Politécnica de Valencia (UPV), for proposing us to participate in this publication.

References

Aguirre LM (2013) Douglas Engelbart (1925–2013), el hombre de la inteligencia. Retrieved 5 Oct 2013, from http://blogs.lavanguardia.com/tecladomovil/douglas-engelbart-1925-2013-el-hombre-de-la-inteligencia-69332

Apple Inc. (2013a) Apple Store. Retrieved from http://store.apple.com/

Apple Inc. (2013b) Apple Store: education. Retrieved from https://itunes.apple.com/es/genre/ios-educacion/id6017?mt=8

Bogost I (2013) The condensed classroom. The Atlantic. Retrieved 26 Nov 2013, from http://www.theatlantic.com/technology/archive/2013/08/the-condensed-classroom/279013/

CERN (2003) Ten years public domain for the original web software. Retrieved from http://tenyears-www.web.cern.ch/tenyears-www/Declaration/Page1.html

Chafkin M (2013) Udacity's Sebastian Thrun, Godfather of free online education, changes course. Fast Company. Retrieved 19 Nov 2013, from http://www.fastcompany.com/3021473/udacity-sebastian-thrun-uphill-climb

Clinton K, Purushotma R, Robison AJ, Weigel M (2006) Confronting the challenges of participatory culture: media education for the 21st century, vol 1. MacArthur Foundation Publication, Chicago, pp 1–59

Cloutier J (1992) EMEREC, la comunicación audio-scripto-visual y la telemediática. In: Silvio J (Comp) Calidad, Tecnología y Globalización en la Educación Superior Latinoamericana. Ediciones CRESALC-UNESCO, Caracas. Retrieved from http://orton.catie.ac.cr/cgi-bin/wxis.exe/?IsisScript=CDIICA.xis&method=post&formato=2&cantidad=1&expresion=mfn=000201

Dailymotion (2011) La guerra por la computadora de uso general empezó (Cory Doctorow). Dailymotion. Retrieved 26 Nov 2013, from http://www.dailymotion.com/video/xnkxe3_cory-doctorow-la-guerra-por-la-computadora-de-uso-general-empezo-revisar-subtitulos_news

Echo 360 (2013) University of North Carolina at Chapel Hill: two published studies on flipping the classroom. Retrieved from http://echo360.com/research-result/university-north-carolina-chapel-hill#sthash.C2RoDjwz.dpufhttp://echo360.com/research-result/university-north-carolina-chapel-hill

Engelbart DC (1962) Augmenting human intellect: a conceptual framework. Retrieved 2 Oct 2013, from http://www.dougengelbart.org/pubs/augment-3906.html

Fried I (2010) Steve jobs: let the post-PC era begin (live blog). Retrieved from http://news.cnet.com/8301-13860_3-20006442-56.html

Google (2013) Google Play. Retrieved from https://play.google.com/store

Jenkins H, Purushotma R, Weigel M, Clinton K, Robison AJ (2009) Confronting the challenges of participatory culture: media education for the 21st century. MIT Press, Cambridge, MA. Retrieved from http://mitpress.mit.edu/sites/default/files/titles/free_download/9780262513623_Confronting_the_Challenges.pdf

Lévy P (2004) Inteligencia Colectiva, por una antropología del ciberespacio: La construcción del ciberespacio. Retrieved from http://inteligenciacolectiva.bvsalud.org/channel.php?channel=1&content=14

Mateos M (2013) Google lanza una versión educativa de la Play Store. Retrieved from http://www.genbeta.com/actualidad/google-lanza-una-version-educativa-de-la-play-store

Miniwatts Marketing Group (2012) Internet world stats: usage and population statistics. Retrieved from http://www.internetworldstats.com/stats.htm

MIT Technology Review (2013) Israel Ruiz (EmTech España). Retrieved from http://es.technologyreview.com/emtech/espana/ponentes/israel-ruiz/

Mitchell W (1997) City of bits. MIT. Retrieved from http://mitpress2.mit.edu/e-books/City_of_Bits/Recombinant_Architecture/index.html

O'Reilly T (2005) What is web 2.0: the architecture of participation. Retrieved from http://oreilly.com/web2/archive/what-is-web-20.html?page=3#designpatterns

Plasencia A (2013) Los Hack del MIT y el aprendizaje. Sistemas informáticos para el aprendizaje ubicuo. Retrieved 7 Oct 2013, from http://aprendizajeubicuo.wordpress.com/2013/04/09/los-hack-del-mit-y-el-aprendizaje/

Rojas N (2013) The faces of Facebook. Retrieved 26 Nov 2013, from http://www.thefacesoffacebook.com

W3C (1990) WorldWideWeb: proposal for a HyperText project. Retrieved from http://www.w3.org/Proposal.html

Wardrip-Fruin N (2004) What hypertext is. Retrieved from http://www.hyperfiction.org/texts/whatHypertextIs.pdf

Wikimedia Foundation (2013) Wikipedia zero. Retrieved from http://wikimediafoundation.org/wiki/Wikipedia_Zero

Chapter 2
Lessons Learned Through Massive Open Online Courses

Mónica López-Sieben, Marta Peris-Ortiz, and Jaime Alonso Gómez

Abstract Despite being a relatively modern educational phenomenon, massive open online courses (MOOCs) are garnering considerable attention in the media, with universities in particular paying heed to these courses because of the opportunity they present.

Broadly speaking, MOOCs are an extension of current long-distance learning courses, and pave the way for new business models that include elements of open education, separating the concepts of teaching and assessment.

Key considerations for the deployment of a MOOC at an educational institution are the course's value proposition, the implementation of an adequate technological platform, the choice of a teaching model to ensure learning, care in maintaining the quality of the course material, recognition of learning acquired by students, and a sustainable business model.

The proliferation of courses run by prestigious institutions offering high-quality open learning material is giving rise to the "universalisation" of knowledge; a scenario in which institutions with lesser repute will increasingly encounter difficulties to compete. Granting students a pivotal role in the education process, and welcoming their influence on the design and orientation of course contents as well as the way

M. López-Sieben (✉)
Centro de Formación Permanente, Universitat Politècnica de València,
Camino de Vera, Valencia 46022, Spain
e-mail: mlopez@cfp.upv.es

M. Peris-Ortiz
Departamento de Organización de Empresas, Universitat Politècnica de València,
Camino de Vera, Valencia 46022, Spain
e-mail: mperis@doe.upv.es

J.A. Gómez
University of San Diego, School of Business, Alcalá Park-Coronado,
San Diego, CA 92110, USA
e-mail: jagomez@itesm.mx

educators adapt learning approaches, may represent a valid strategy in the quest for differentiation in a highly competitive environment.

2.1 Introduction

Massive open online courses (MOOCs) embody an educational process that serves a huge number of people worldwide, and that has sparked massive interest from governments, educational institutions, and commercial enterprises. Following their boom in popularity some years ago, a large number of platforms offering university-affiliated and unaffiliated MOOCs have sprung up. More and more institutions are beginning to experiment with MOOCs, with the aim of widening access, promoting the institution and its brand, and discovering a way of augmenting sources of financing for the future (Yuan and Powell 2013).

MOOCs are defined as long-distance courses devised for a large number of students (in theory, unlimited), that are open, global, and participative.

The term "open" is a key concept nowadays. The two most important aspects of the open concept have to do with making content fully available over the Internet, and imposing the fewest possible restrictions on students in terms of requiring technical, legal, and financial resources (OECD 2008).

In general, these courses are free of charge. Nonetheless, in the medium term, institutions can generate some kind of income if, for instance, students wish to obtain certificates recognising their participation in these courses.

For students, the lure of learning in dynamic surroundings from top academics, together with these courses' backing from renowned educational institutions, gives MOOCs a strong value proposition that is worthy of further examination. Meanwhile, for institutions, the chance of gaining direct access to a group of students who have already demonstrated a sufficient degree of involvement during the course offers numerous advantages associated with cross-selling to this collective and the value of these students' feedback to help plan subsequent editions of the course.

2.1.1 History and Key Features of MOOCs

The term massive open online course (MOOC) was coined in 2008 by Dave Cormier (2008) to refer to the course, "Connectivism and Connective Knowledge [CCK08]", at the University of Manitoba (Canada), led by the lecturers George Siemens and Stephen Downes. This course was offered to 25 official students, and some 2,300 additional students participated free of charge on an open basis.

Some time afterwards, Sebastian Thrun and his colleagues at Stanford University provided open access to the standard university course, "Introduction to Artificial Intelligence", on which 160,000 students from 190 countries enrolled.

Since then, many higher education institutions that wish to keep pace with other prestigious establishments and emulate them as they ride the popularity wave of this educational phenomenon have adopted MOOCs.

MOOCs are free to access, open to an unlimited number of participants, generally offer no qualification for participants paying no fee, and run from a technological platform that enables the distribution of course material and appraisal of students.

On the other hand, connective MOOCs (cMOOCs), such as that of Siemens and Downes, consist of an instructional design that seeks to create discussion and participation amongst students. This approach places the student and the connections made during the course at the centre of the learning process, which means that enrolees can follow their own learning roadmap and are in fact responsible for creating the majority of the course material.

Conversely, Thurn's (Udacity, Coursera, Edx, etc.) non-connectivist MOOCs, or xMOOCs, rely on contents that have the backing of the host institution, and that essentially consist of self-study and self-assessment material, which somewhat restricts students' freedom to determine which direction the course will take.

2.2 Implementing MOOCs at an Educational Institution

Institutions wishing to implement a MOOCs project must devise a strategy that covers six main areas:

1. *Implementation strategy and value proposition*: What is the underlying strategic aim of an institutions' decision to implement a MOOCs project, and what value do these courses add for the student?
2. *Technology platform*: What are the features and functionalities offered by the technology platform for these courses?
3. *Teaching model*: What is the underlying teaching model that guarantees the best learning experience for students of the course?
4. *Quality of course material*: How does the institution ensure the quality of the courses they offer, and how does it plan to update and continually improve the course material? What communication strategy does the institution wish to implement to keep students informed?
5. *Accreditation and recognition*: What are the assessment procedures to evaluate knowledge acquired, and what type of recognition do the course qualifications hold? How does the university verify the identity of users?
6. *Financing model*: How does the institution ensure long-term sustainability of the project without comprising the premise of free access for users?

2.2.1 Implementation Strategy and Value Proposition

The implementation of a series of MOOCs may serve as a brand-placement strategy—especially for public institutions and non-profit organisations—that stresses the idea of a commitment to society and advanced technological capabilities. Nevertheless, once the project is in motion and has achieved its initial impact, the financing model must undergo a re-evaluation to ensure the project's long-term sustainability.

For students, free access to high-quality courses and course content, and the permanent acquisition of new skills that are necessary for personal and professional development make up one of the fundamental value propositions. The following factors may also be combined with the above value proposal:

- "One-click" access to free, high-quality long-distance learning.
- Sharing or granting certain firms access to the profiles of students from all over the world who have knowledge in a specific area. This process boosts employment.
- Leading institutions' recognition of the training or competencies acquired (following some kind of specific assessment method).
- Access, in the user's own language, to courses from leading institutions.

For the institution, in addition to the aforementioned potential for brand placement, the implementation of MOOCs yields the following opportunities:

- Use of data about students to carry out studies of demand and consumer trends in the areas where they are most necessary.
- Improvement of the virtual platform, and creation and contextualisation of course contents based on students' feedback.
- Students' awareness of the institution and its teaching methodology as a potential destination for subsequent (paying) study.

This steady universalisation of knowledge through courses run by renowned institutions will create a tipping point within the market and a reduction in the academic offer, in the sense that less well-known institutions will encounter difficulties in attracting students to the courses they offer. At this point, it will be crucial for institutions to establish differentiated value propositions and blue ocean strategies for their survival in such a competitive market.

2.2.2 Technology Platform

When deciding on a technology platform to deploy MOOCs, institutions may opt to develop or use their own platform, or offer their course via an external platform that maintains the identity of the host institution. In any event, the technology platform must have, amongst others, the following features:

- The platform must be robust enough to allow efficient access to large numbers of students simultaneously, autonomously, and at any time of day or night.
- The interface must be user-friendly to encourage learning and retention on the part of the students.
- The platform should have an advertising and client-capture system, based on viral systems that operate via social networks, online marketing, web placement, and the like, to ensure growth in the number of users.
- The platform should include student–student and student–lecturer forums and areas to post comments, as well as automatic self-assessment systems (both amongst peers and through personal assessment from the tutor).

- Security measures to control access to contents and personal details of the participants. Definition and use of different licensing options (e.g., creative commons) for content sharing and source verification.
- Personalised tools to monitor students' individual learning progress.

2.2.3 Teaching Model

To attract and retain users, institutions offering MOOCs should take the following strategic actions:

- Establishment of templates and guidelines for the production of materials, along with the quality, duration, and size of videos, presentations, and documents, and their review and appraisal.
- Implementation of user interaction functionalities, for both the educator and other users, through forums, chat rooms, video tutorials, meeting points for local groups, wikis, and so forth.
- Development of tools for lecturers to assign marks to students. This may involve either implementing peer-assessment systems, or automatic appraisal systems (intelligent tutoring) based on statistical tracking of students' responses to assessment exercises.
- Evolution of the teaching model from a single, standard model for all students to a connective, cooperative model that each student can customise as he or she sees fit.

2.2.4 Quality of Course Material

To ensure the quality and relevance of the course contents, institutions should pay heed to the following considerations:

- Initial review of the contents for the MOOCs on offer and the level of eminence of the associated academic faculty.
- Setting up appropriate user assessment systems to obtain students' feedback, using end-of-course questionnaires, complaints and suggestions boxes, forums with specific questions, and other such tools.
- Incentives for lecturers to update and improve course contents on a regular basis. Attempts to engage in the program faculty members with international standing.
- International accreditation of courses, if applicable.
- Detection of the real market needs to allow institutions to channel, adjust, and extend their offer.
- Implementation of access to sources, databases and open resources on the world stage to support the promotion of the courses.

Table 2.1 Costs associated with the implementation of MOOCs

	Technology	Curriculum
Set-up costs	Cost of implementing the platform to offer MOOCs and monitor students' progress	Cost of production of new materials
Operating costs	Cost of maintenance and upkeep of the platform	Cost of delivering courses and assessing enrolees
		Cost of updating course material
		Cost of distributing course material

Source: Authors' own work

2.2.5 Accreditation and Recognition

Institutions should consider the following issues relating to the accreditation and recognition of their MOOCs students:

- Design of robust learning assessment systems that allow easy identification of competencies acquired. Establishing mechanisms for checking and correcting unclear or borderline progress tests.
- Establishing procedures that allow the verification of the identity of students in progress tests that are academically or institutionally well recognised.
- Setting up institutional alliances that allow students to receive accreditation for learning even if it takes place outside the classroom, bridging the gap between formal, non-formal, and informal education.

2.2.6 Financing Model

More than "free" education, MOOCs are about education that, in reality, is "free, but not free". In education, as in other sectors where firms are developing a supply of free goods and services, surviving enterprises and institutions look for indirect ways of covering the costs that always underlie this type of venture (Cusumano 2013).

To ensure a long-term, sustainable supply of free courses, it is important to bear in mind that such a venture induces certain costs, as Table 2.1 shows.

2.2.6.1 Set-up Costs

The costs of setting up a robust platform for running MOOCs along with the production of long-distance course materials is a considerable barrier to entry for institutions without the existing infrastructure and material, especially given that MOOCs are essentially free for enrolment. At this juncture, and depending on the

Table 2.2 Set-up costs

Cost of setting up the platform to offer MOOCs and monitoring students' progress
• Institutional or endowment: the sponsor institution makes the initial investment (e.g., EdX)
• Governmental: support from the government if this is a strategically important area
• Strategic alliance: the institution forms a strategic alliance with an existing platform that possesses the necessary technological capability and wishes to expand its range of services (e.g., collaboration with the MiriadaX on the Universia platform)
Cost of producing new material for long-distance learning courses
• Institutional or endowment: the host institution makes an investment in support teams who help faculty prepare material for the courses. In some cases, the institution also offers financial compensation for experts who produce course material
• Governmental: (Ever decreasing) government subsidies for producing study material for long-distance courses
• Model "paid for" by the producer: the lecturer invests his time into the production (without generating expert costs), normally either expecting to recover the investment through subsequent leveraging of the course, or because of altruism. Lecturers may receive intangible benefits such as a reduction in their teaching workload, taking into account the final assessment and promotion, etc.

Source: Author's own work, drawing on de Langen and Bitter-Rijkema (2012), Dholakia et al. (2006), Downes (2007), and Herrera (2010)

particular case, the institution must decide between implementing or using its own platform, and whether to produce new contents for the courses or to re-use existing material (Table 2.2).

2.2.6.2 Operating Costs

The operating costs, albeit lower than set-up costs, are significant and exert a considerable influence on the end satisfaction of the users, as well as their retention and the sustainability of the project. Table 2.3 presents an overview of the main ways of raising funds to cover these costs.

It is no longer simply a case of covering costs, but rather an opportunity for the institution to exploit an additional income stream.

2.3 Key Examples of Implementation of Open Resources and MOOCs

Table 2.4 shows a summary of the analysis of some leading institutions that implement MOOCs, their financing models (Benkler 2005, 2006) and the way they conduct the courses (Downes 2007), as well as their chosen financing model (OECD 2008):

Table 2.3 Operating costs

Cost of platform maintenance and updates
• Institutional: the sponsor institution continues to provide support to the project for strategic reasons (e.g., EdX)
• Membership model: certain institutions pay regular fees for the maintenance of the portal. This may be the case for portals developed to host courses from several institutions (e.g., universities' membership in Universia)
• Alliances and exchanges: with the use of open platforms, volunteers from all over the world can collaborate and contribute to the free development of new functionalities on the platform, and thus achieve systematic maintenance of the system
Cost of delivering courses and monitoring students' progress
Cost of updating contents
Cost of distributing course material
• Endowment model: through donations from those who are interested in maintaining the project (e.g., Khan Academy). This model has limited penetration in Spain
• Conversion model: the first module of a course is available free of charge, in the hope that subscribers will pay the inscription fee for additional courses
• Substitution model: this is a cost reduction model more than a financing model. For example, this model avoids the costs of transport for lecturers of long-distance learning courses with global scope
• "Self-Paid" model: Faculty members seek other non-monetary advantages to giving up their time for this initiative (e.g., publicity and international exposure)
• Segmentation model: courses are free but additional services have a charge (e.g., certificate, consultancy services, book sales, etc.)
• Alliances and exchanges: collaboration with other entities in the production and exchange of resources maintains or extends the range of courses on offer
• Sponsorship model: once the course achieves a large user base, the platform can integrate advertisements into the course contents, or seek out a sponsor interested in the courses on offer (e.g., Universia and Santander Bank)

Source: Author's own work, drawing on de Langen and Bitter-Rijkema (2012), Dholakia et al. (2006), Downes (2007), and Herrera (2010)

2.4 Conclusions

Online education, technology capable of disseminating large quantities of knowledge in multiple formats, and the possibility of handling mass course inscriptions have all been ready for deployment for many years. Only with the rise in popularity of MOOCs, however, have these advances begun to receive serious attention.

The proliferation of MOOCs has left the market wide open, breaking down the barriers of distance and the institutional hurdles to bring high-quality, global knowledge sharing (institutional backing) to a large audience (massive), without access restrictions (open), and for next to no cost (free). This will bring about, "a genuine transformation of the system, stemming from a greater impact of the principle of supply and demand in an increasingly globalised environment" (Leal 2008).

For students, the chance to gain free, open access to the top academics from prestigious institutions in a dynamic environment, and share experiences with other students from all four corners of the world represents huge value added.

Table 2.4 Implementation models of relevant institutions

	Type of institution	Provider of course	Role of the student as a contributor	Financing model
MIT OCW. ocw.mit.edu/index.htm	Non-profit	Institution	Producer–consumer	Institutional donation
Khan Academy. www.khanacademy.org	Non-profit	Institution	Producer–consumer	Donation
Udacity. www.udacity.com	For-profit	Institution	Producer–consumer	Segmentation (charge for certificates) Donation
Coursera. www.coursera.org	For-profit	Institution	Producer–consumer	Segmentation (charge for certificates)
EdX. www.edx.org	Non-profit	Institution	Producer–consumer	Institutional Alliances and exchanges (maintaining the open platform with collaborators)
TED. www.ted.com		Institution Donation	Producer–consumer Donation	Annual membership
TED-ED. Ed.ted.com		Community Donation	Producer–consumer	Annual membership
Udemy. www.udemy.com	For-profit	Community	Producer–consumer	Segmentation
ITunes U. www.apple.com/es/education/itunes-u/	For-profit	Community	Producer–consumer	Institutional
P2PU. p2pu.org/en	Non-profit	Community	Co-producer	
The University of the people. www.uopeople.org	Non-profit	Community	Co-producer	Institutional donation Segmentation (charge for student's file and exams)

Source: Authors' own work

For an institution, on the other hand, making contact with highly motivated, participative international students, presents a huge opportunity to extend its brand on the world stage, capture new students, and, additionally, test and develop innovative learning initiatives in virtual environments.

To implement a MOOCs project, an institution must set a clear strategy in the following areas: (a) implementation and value proposition; (b) capabilities of the technology platform; (c) underlying educational model; (d) quality of the course material; (e) assessment and accreditation model; and (f) a business financing model that ensures the sustainability of the project.

In this scenario, knowledge is becoming "universal", and prominent institutions are developing high-quality open contents. Therefore, it will be difficult to compete and find a niche in the market without offering services with differentiated value propositions. In this battle, the repute of the institution will be of the utmost importance. It is highly probable that non-elite educational institutions will be unable to survive in this new environment (Cusumano 2013).

Currently, possibilities still exist to offer non-English courses, but the ease of translating course material weakens this advantage.

Another unresolved area has to do with the universalisation of knowledge. This process somewhat overlooks the effect of the multicultural nature of the global student body in terms of considering diverse habits and customs in different parts of the world. Thus, the contextualisation of course material is a pending issue.

The large potential for development lies in the innovation in learning processes, placing students at the centre of the learning process as the determiners and co-creators of their own learning roadmap (Benkler 2005, 2006).

In this sense, the tendency to move away from xMOOCs towards cMOOCs is one of the areas in which prestigious institutions are deploying their strategies. In these cases, therefore, learning grows continuously with reference to other experts, other cultures, other experiences, and other communities with the same interests.

Recognition, by institutions or businesses, of the competencies and skills acquired by each student and the adaptation of the learning channels leads to a more individual and customised education. The support of technology in MOOCs makes it possible to carry out a personal assessment of each student's progress (Cooper and Sahami 2013).

Educational institutions must evolve from their current form—centres where teachers merely impart knowledge—by adopting a role as the student's partner. This partnership means guiding students on how to develop their knowledge of a subject, and teaching students to pick out relevant, reliable sources to conduct their own learning.

Acknowledgements Research reported in this paper was supported by Universitat Politècnica de València (Spain) Project PIME A07-13.

References

Benkler Y (2005) Common wisdom: peer production of educational materials. The Center for Open and Sustainable Learning, Utah State University. Available from www.benkler.org/Common_Wisdom.pdf

Benkler Y (2006) The wealth of networks. How social production transforms markets and freedom. Yale University Press, New Haven and London

Cooper S, Sahami M (2013) Reflections on Standford's MOOCs. Commun ACM 56(2):28–30

Cormier D (2008) The CCK08 MOOC—connectivism course, 1/4 way. Dave's Educational Blog. Available from http://davecormier.com/edblog/2008/10/02/the-cck08-mooc-connectivism-course-14-way/

Cusumano MA (2013) Are the costs of "free" too high in online education? Commun ACM 56(4):26–29

De Langen FHT, Bitter-Rijkema ME (2012) Positioning the OER business model for open education. Eur J Open Distance E-Learning vol. I. Available from http://www.eurodl.org/index.php?article=483. Accessed 7 March 2012

Dholakia UM, King WJ, Baraniuk R (2006) What makes an open education program sustainable? The case of connections. Available from www.oecd.org/dataoecd/3/6/36781781.pdf

Downes S (2007) Models for sustainable open educational resources. Interdiscip J Knowl Learn Objects 3:29–44. Available from http://ijello.org/Volume3/IJKLOv3p029-044Downes.pdf

Herrera S (2010) Open educational resources: how can open education programs be sustainable? Knowledge 2(1). Available from http://ojs.stanford.edu/ojs/index.php/a2k/article/viewFile/425/251

Leal D (2008) Una revisión de "El Futuro de la Educación" de Thomas Frey (Parte 1). Edu. Co.Blog. Available from http://www.diegoleal.org/social/blog/blogs/index.php/2008/01/12/thomas-frey-the-future-of-education?blog=2

OECD (2008) El conocimiento libre y los recursos educativos abiertos. OECD, Organización para la cooperación y el desarrollo económicos. Available from http://www.oecd.org/edu/ceri/42281358.pdf

Yuan L, Powell S (2013) MOOCs and open education: implications for higher education. A white paper. JISC CETIS. Centre for Educational Technology & Interoperatibility Standards, United Kindom. Available from http://publications.cetis.ac.uk/wp-content/uploads/2013/03/MOOCs-and-Open-Education.pdf

Chapter 3
Integration of Virtual Teaching/Learning Environments in Higher Education for the Development of Formative Assessment in the Field of Accounting

Adelaida Ciudad-Gómez, Jesús Valverde-Berrocoso, and José Luis Coca-Pérez

Abstract So-called "virtual campuses" are mainly used by universities with "blended learning" systems, which involve a combination of face-to-face instruction and learning by digital means. "Blended learning" is at the heart of a transformation of the teaching/learning process in higher education, for it opens up the possibility of generating a community of inquiry and learning beyond the face-to-face classroom. The European Higher Education Area framework has given students the lead role in the new educational scenario in a model in which the use of information and communications technology along with active learning methodologies is facilitating competency-based learning, autonomous use of educational resources and collaborative work, as well as a development of formative assessment allowing for suitable assessment frequency and providing useful feedback, enhancing students' motivation and academic performance.

This chapter presents an experience of educational innovation in Financial Accounting and describes the pedagogical design of a subject in "blended learning" format focussed on students' learning activity and on a competency-based assessment strategy.

3.1 Introduction: Blended Learning and Assessment for Learning in Higher Education

International research on assessment for learning in higher education has greatly developed over the past decade. Processes of reform in universities have been linked to a reflection on the nature of assessment and have allowed fruitful development in

A. Ciudad-Gómez (✉) • J.L. Coca-Pérez
Accounting and Financial Economy Department, University of Extremadura,
Avda. de la Universidad, Cáceres 10071, Spain
e-mail: adelaida@unex.es; jlcoca@unex.es

J. Valverde-Berrocoso
Department of Education, University of Extremadura,
Avda. de la Universidad, Cáceres 10071, Japan
e-mail: jevabe@unex.es

specialist research in these areas. There is agreement across the scientific community on the need to improve the quality of university students' learning outcomes, for which innovations in assessment are essential (Boud and Falchikov 2006).

Nowadays "sustainable assessment" is advocated, able to meet learning needs in the present without compromising students' ability to meet learning needs in the future. Sustainable assessment covers the knowledge, skills and aptitudes required to support lifelong learning.

"Learning-oriented assessment" is also advocated, basically consisting of active student participation, feed-forward and "authentic" tasks. This is a theoretical construct based on university practice which uses assessment strategies that promote and maximise students' learning opportunities. Its purpose is to develop useful competencies of value to the academic present and the working future (Ibarra et al. 2012).

We should also consider the profile of students currently entering university, characterised by what has been conceptualised as a "digital generation", and this requires changes in conventional relationships in educational environments between students themselves and between students and teachers, facilitating collaborative, decentralised and plural learning (Rowlands and Nicholas 2008).

From the institutional sphere, features of best practice in competency assessment are: (1) a syllabus design agreed on the basis of the competencies defined for each occupational profile; (2) a collegiate organisation linked to the subject goals; (3) an explicit assessment design agreed both for the subject and for the degree course; (4) an assessment design linked across the various subjects working on the same competencies; (5) shared or joint assessment going beyond the unit of any one subject; (6) assessment integrating different competencies; (7) an integration and application of learning in experiences reflecting the world of work; (8) assessment consistent with or adapted to pedagogical design; (9) diagnostic assessment, on the understanding that acquiring competencies is a progressive process; (10) formative assessment which ensures that students know their strengths and weaknesses; (11) varied assessment on the basis of various marking techniques and instruments; (12) multi-agent assessment: self-assessment and co-assessment together with hetero-assessment; (13) assessment that generates learning; and (14) significant and motivating assessment (Tierno et al. 2013).

At the heart of this transformation of the teaching/learning processes in higher education is the use of "blended learning" (BL), for this opens up the possibility of generating a community of inquiry and learning beyond the face-to-face classroom (Marqués et al. 2011), a form of virtual campus combining face-to-face instruction with delivery by digital means.

The experts believe that BL is set to become the most widely applied model in higher education (Garrison and Vaughan 2013). BL also involves a restructuring of face-to-face space-time organisation in universities so as to encourage access to the learning opportunities offered by virtual environments. It also involves a transformation of the traditional teaching/learning approach. Consequently some researchers hold that BL is a "dangerous idea", for it challenges the *status quo*, maintaining the integrity of the traditional academic system while simultaneously promoting the use of e-learning platforms, mobile technologies and resources "in the cloud" (Moskal et al. 2013).

The basic principle of BL is that face-to-face oral communication and online written communication are integrated so that they "blend" into a single learning experience, consistent with the context and the educational goals.

Three stages may be defined in the adoption of BL in a university (Graham et al. 2013): (1) awareness/exploration, (2) adoption/early implementation, and (3) mature implementation/growth. Universities at the "exploration" stage initially use BL as a means of resolving certain problems or challenges that they face as higher education institutions: rapid growth in certain courses or centres, the wish to cater for as many students as possible, insufficient physical infrastructure, the wish to make the teaching/learning process more flexible or the need to optimise human, material and financial resources, among others. Universities at the "adoption" stage are geared to implementing innovations that allow them to update their organisational structures so as to adapt to a digital environment and include more flexible course offerings. They focus on establishing well-defined procedures for the pedagogical design of BL courses and start to provide initiatives for lecturers. Assessment of learning outcomes is still incipient and little developed. Finally universities that have reached the "growth" stage offer BL courses fully integrated and mainstreamed in their academic offering, and work on continuous improvement through systematic assessment and data mining, which helps them to take strategic internal decisions.

As to the key features of developing BL in higher education, Garrison and Vaughan (2013) highlight: (a) fully re-conceptualising and redesigning the subject or course, (b) suitably managing the information volume, and (c) creating a community of learning and inquiry so as to take advantage of what we know of higher learning experiences and the properties of communication with digital technologies.

One of the most significant steps to be taken by a university using BL is that of providing procedures and structures for gathering data for the purpose of thoroughly monitoring and systematically evaluating the effects of decisions and steps taken regarding BL. Only with exhaustive information gathering is it possible to answer questions relating, for example, to the effects of BL on students' learning (Garrison and Vaughan 2013).

Student satisfaction is a key factor in evaluating quality in a BL experience, and in this respect students demand that the design of BL subjects or courses include the following features (del Moral and Villalustre 2009): a clear definition of learning goals; hierarchical, contextualised and consistently structured presentation of contents; diverse individual and group activities; a thorough account of assessment criteria in keeping with the goals set; and the creation of windows for individual tutoring. Moreover, communication is a key feature in substituting the loss of face-to-face contact with efficient use of tools for synchronous and asynchronous interaction (Aznar et al. 2009).

It has been shown that students have a positive predisposition towards BL and high expectations as to its potential for enhancing learning (Area et al. 2008; Cabero and Llorente 2009). And that, furthermore, using BL has positive effects in reducing the dropout rate from university subjects and on learning outcomes. Including BL learning activities has positive effects on students' final grades. And BL tasks enrich face-to-face activities without needing to wholly replace them (López et al. 2011).

However, it is higher-performing students that express most satisfaction with this form of learning, given its flexibility, the higher motivation for learning that it generates and its contribution to a better understanding of key concepts in subjects (Owston et al. 2013).

3.2 Methodology in the Design of Our Blended Learning Proposal

The design of the BL subject "Financial Accounting III" (Table 3.1), subject belonging to the *Accounting* module of the syllabus for a *Degree in Business Administration and Management*, in the *Learning Management Systems*—LMS (Moodle) implemented in the Virtual Campus of Extremadura University (CVUEx).

The aim was to provide a tool to support our competency-based education and assessment model *management of competence in the areas of Accounting* (MANCOMA) (Ciudad and Valverde 2012) and to enable us to develop a teaching/learning process in a virtual environment suited to individual needs so as to foster autonomy and student activity to encourage the development of competencies specific to the discipline and generic to the degree course (Fig. 3.1).

Before the BL subject was designed, the competencies were standardised (with definition of sub-competencies and indicators), scoring rubrics were drawn up and activities were devised for developing competencies and documenting knowledge and performance. On its transfer to the LMS, the subject was structured into five modules.

Table 3.1 Profile of the course "Financial Accounting III"

Course	Financial Accounting III
Syllabus	Degree in Business Administration and Management (BAM)
Modulo	3. Accounting
Material	3.1. Financial Accounting
Type of course	Obligatory Type 1
Centre	Faculty of Business and Tourism Studies—*University of Extremadura* (Spain)
Level of the unit and term	The second year and two second semester
Number of ECTS credits	Six credits
Descriptors	Train students in the formulation, presentation and understanding of Financial Statements, especially those that must be formulated periodically in accordance with national and international accounting rules, i.e. the Annual Accounts and Interim Financial Statements that may be requested by any current or potential user
Groups and number of students	BAM-A group: 103 students BAM-B group: 89 students

Source: Curriculum of Business Administration and Management

3 Integration of Virtual Teaching/Learning Environments in Higher Education...

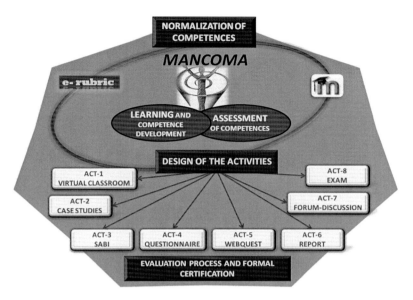

Fig. 3.1 Management of competence in the areas of accounting

Table 3.2 Structure of the virtual course "Financial Accounting III"

Modules	Items
I	Presentation of the course
II	Item 1: Course syllabus
III	Item 2: Theory of the course
IV	Item 3: Supplementary material
V. Training and assessment activities	Item 4: ACT-1. Virtual classroom
	Item 5: ACT-2. Case studies
	Item 6: ACT-3. SABI
	Item 7: ACT-4. Questionnaire
	Item 8: ACT-5. *WebQuest*
	Item 9: ACT-6. Report
	Item 10: ACT-7. Forum-discussion
	Item 11: ACT-8. Objective test (exam)

In the first module there is a presentation of the subject, the communication forums and a survey; the second contains the syllabus; the third, theory documents drawn up by the lecturer; the fourth, links to web resources or documents; and the fifth, educational and assessment activities to be done by students. To this last module we give special attention below (Table 3.2).

In the BL subject's module of teaching and assessment activities, in line with the competencies to be developed, a series of strategies and instruments were combined so as to document evidence of both knowledge and performance via face-to-face and online activities, for which a topic was devoted to each one.

To each activity the following resources were added: the activity sheet, the rubric, a URL with the GTEA (https://gteavirtual.org/rubric/) *eRubric* tool, used to log self-assessment and peer assessment, *file-upload* tasks for students' deliverables, and *offline activity* tasks for tutor assessment.

Moreover ACT-1 included a poll for the choice of a group by students and a forum to allow each group to report on its choice of coordinator, and ACT-2 used *offline activity* tasks to allow inclusion of grades from face-to-face tests outside the virtual subject and attendance control. Moreover, a self-assessment test was added as a *questionnaire* activity for ACT-4 with the aim of instructing and assessing students on certain required contents and enabling them to get their results in real time.

In ACT-5 we used a methodology widely applied in recent years in various educational environments created by Dodge (1995), which maintains that students will be able to build their own learning if the teacher, taking the role of mediator, provides the necessary cognitive scaffolding. A WebQuest is defined as "An inquiry-oriented activity in which most or all of the information used by learners is drawn from the Web. WebQuests are designed to use learners' time well, to focus on using information rather than looking for it, and to support learners' thinking at the levels of analysis, synthesis, and evaluation" (Dodge 1997).

The activity was designed in the first place as a website using an HTML editor, then it was converted into a SCORM package with *reload-editor*, a content package and metadata editor and a suitable tool for transforming our WebQuest activity and giving it a standard structure readable to the LMS (Moodle), conveniently storing all the files required in a single .zip archive.

In ACT-7 students are offered a question for discussion and debate. In its design we considered consistency with learning goals, the debate's functionality in the teaching/learning process, establishing a debating calendar, choice of forum mode (LMS options), agreed rules and principles governing debates and the need to introduce complementary materials.

Finally ACT-8 is the test that students have to take on the official exam day, so the BL subject includes the activity sheet and rubric for the activity and an *offline* task so that the grades scored in the activity may be included. This is a face-to-face test.

3.3 Conclusions

In the design and creation of the BL subject we used an LMS (Moodle) allowing us to distribute documents in various formats, administer discussion forums, give online access to files, videos and sites, create work groups, offer assessable teaching activities online, organise a student's diary with key tasks and dates and posting of notices, and monitor each individual student's access to the platform.

In designing our BL unit we adopted certain initial *pedagogical* and *technological* approaches according to the content, competencies and goals involved, and to the profile of the students taking the course. Implementing our teaching activity and deploying the BL subject allowed us to combine distance and face-to-face methodology, marrying a dialectical method, with the resolving of practical cases, with a heuristic method, with individual and group activities. We developed an environment geared to self-regulated learning in which the rubrics became a suitable tool for providing useful feedback to students and allowing self-assessment and peer assessment, helping to make students more autonomous and fostering collaborative and cooperative work.

We are analysing the results and contributions from this experience so as to appraise the extent to which this pedagogical innovation has enhanced quality in the teaching of accounting subjects.

References

Area M, Sanabria AL, González M (2008) Análisis de una experiencia de docencia universitaria semipresencial desde la perspectiva del alumnado. RIED: Revista Iberoamericana de Educación a Distancia 11(1):231–254
Aznar I, Hinojo FJ, Cáceres MP (2009) Percepciones del alumnado sobre el blended learning en la universidad. Comunicar: Revista científica iberoamericana de comunicación y educación 33:165–174
Boud D, Falchikov N (2006) Aligning assessment with long-term learning. Assess Eval High Educ 31(4):399–413
Cabero J, Llorente MC (2009) Actitudes, satisfacción, rendimiento académico y comunicación online en procesos de formación universitaria en blended learning. Teoría de la Educación: Educación y Cultura en la Sociedad de la Información 10(1):172–189
Ciudad A, Valverde J (2012) Design of a competency-based assessment model in the field of accounting. Contemp Issues Educ Res 5(5):343–348. Available from http://journals.cluteonline.com/index.php/CIER/article/view/7466/7532. Accessed Dec 2012
del Moral ME, Villalustre L (2009) Proyecto M.A.T.R.I.X.: modalidades de aprendizaje telemático y resultados interuniversitarios extrapolables al blended learning. RIED: Revista Iberoamericana de Educación a Distancia 12(2):163–187
Dodge B (1995) Webquest: a technique for internet-based learning. Distance Educ 1(2):10–13
Dodge B (1997) Some thoughts about webquests. Available from http://webquest.sdsu.edu/about_webquests.html. Accessed Dec 2012
Garrison DR, Vaughan ND (2013) Institutional change and leadership associated with blended learning innovation: two case studies. Internet High Educ 18:24–28
Graham CR, Woodfield W, Harrison JB (2013) A framework for institutional adoption and implementation of blended learning in higher education. Internet High Educ 18:4–14
Ibarra MS, Rodríguez G, y Gómez MA (2012) La evaluación entre iguales: Beneficios y estrategias para su práctica en la universidad. Revista de Educación 359. Available from http://www.revistaeducacion.mec.es/doi/359_092.pdf. Accessed Feb 2013
López MV, Pérez MC, Rodríguez L (2011) Blended learning in higher education: students' perceptions and their relation to outcomes. Comput Educ 56(3):818–826
Marqués L, Espuny C, González J, Gisbert M (2011) La creación de una comunidad aprendizaje en una experiencia de blended learning. Pixel-Bit: Revista de medios y educación 39:55–68
Moskal P, Dziuban C, Hartman J (2013) Blended learning: a dangerous idea? Internet High Educ 18:15–23
Owston R, York D, Murtha S (2013) Student perceptions and achievement in a university blended learning strategic initiative. Internet High Educ 18:38–46
Rowlands I, Nicholas D (2008) Information behaviour of the researcher of the future. University College of London, London
Tierno JM, Iranzo P, y Barrios C (2013) El compromiso organizativo e institucional para diseñar y evaluar competencias en la universidad. Revista de Educación 361:223–251. doi: 10-4438/1988-592X-RE-2011-361-141. Available from http://www.mecd.gob.es/dctm/revista-de-educacion/articulosre361/re36109.pdf?documentId=0901e72b8162f032. Accessed Oct 2013

Chapter 4
Developing Moral Competence in Higher Education

Manuel Guillén, Michael O'Mara Shimek, and Ernesto de los Reyes

Abstract In the European Qualifications Framework (EQF), moral and ethical competence is nearly absent from curricula development criteria. The recovery and incorporation of moral competence is an essential reflection: by integrating the ethical or moral dimensions of knowledge with the intellectual and technical dimensions, higher education can more effectively respond to the needs of society. This chapter affirms that the concept of habit offers an innovative perspective on human behavior that can contribute towards a more complete understanding and development of the concept of competence, and specifically of "moral competence" for both the sciences and social sciences.

M. Guillén (✉)
Management Department & IECO-UNESCO Chair (UV-UPV),
University of Valencia School of Economics, Avd. de los Naranjos, 46022 Valencia,
Valencia, Spain
e-mail: Manuel.Guillen@uv.es

M.O. Shimek
School of Education and Sports, Catholic University of Valencia,
C/Sagrado Corazón, 46110 Godella, Valencia, Spain
e-mail: Michael.Omara@ucv.es

E. de los Reyes
Institute of Innovation and Knowledge Management, INGENIO (CSIC-UPV),
Polytechnic University of Valencia, Camino de Vera,
46022 Valencia, Valencia, Spain
e-mail: ede@ingenio.upv.es

4.1 Introduction[1]

Today's social and economic challenges call for university graduates with strong moral competence. In higher education, two options exist for instructors: we can either perpetuate traditional methods and continue to lament the lack of moral values in society, or we can innovate. By integrating the ethical or moral dimensions of knowledge with the intellectual and technical dimensions, this chapter proposes an alternative approach to how higher education can more effectively respond to the needs of society.

Knowledge has effects in different realms. It not only develops theoretical or scientific dimensions, or *knowing*, but also practical, technical, and artistic ones, or knowing *how to do* something. Knowledge, however, also has an ethical or moral dimension reflected in how human conduct is judged, or knowing *how to act (or live)* (Guillén et al. 2007). This chapter urges students in general, and university students in particular, to learn by acquiring not only intellectual and technical skills but also ethical habits, or moral competence.

Although various international authorities have insisted on the importance of ethical learning in higher education for future professionals during the process of creating the European Higher Education Area, and a common European Qualifications Framework (EQF), consideration given to ethical qualifications has been curtailed and subjected to serious limitations (Guillén et al. 2007). In a book devoted to innovation and teaching technologies, we consider the recovery and incorporation of moral competence in university curricula to be an essential reflection: if ethics is not explicitly taken into account throughout the educational process, the result is likely to produce graduates who have no notion of the rules of professional conduct, nor of the virtues they should have in order to follow those rules.

Training in moral competence does not imply a "zero sum" result, or a reduction in the preparation of the other technical and intellectual competences. On the contrary, both prove highly synergistic for both students and instructors: students find greater meaning in technical training giving them greater motivation and increasing their dedication. At the same time, instructors discover a higher meaning in teaching. This provides them with greater satisfaction which serves to enliven their own dedication and strengthen their efforts (Finkel 2000).

4.2 The Concept of Moral Competence

To define moral competence, one must first come to an understanding of morality. Morality or ethics has to do with the right and proper completion of a person with human excellence through rational judgment and practical action. "The moral dimension demands a kind of moral or ethical learning understood as the acquisition

---

[1] The three authors of this work are members of the Institute for Ethics in Communication and Organizations (IECO). www.ieco.us

of theoretical moral principles of conduct and of practical moral virtues" (Guillén 2006). Moral competence, therefore, could be described as the possession of certain principles or behavioral norms for achieving good ethics, combined with practical habits for personal improvement (Bañón Gomis et al. 2012). While total agreement does not exist concerning the definition of a technical or intellectual competence, there is more and more of a consensus in describing it as a body of observable habitual behaviors that make it possible for a person to be successful in one's job or professional responsibilities (Cardona and García-Lombardía 2005). It is a question of developing the habits that make a professional technically and intellectually excellent. Some of these habits include the capacity to organize one's responsibilities, to benchmark, to set realistic objectives, and to engage in teamwork, among others. We argue that these competences or habits are inseparable from other habits which are also observable. These habits have more to do with being able to work in the service of others than towards the success of specific actions or projects. Such habits are more concerned with the personal improvement of those who carry them out and the improvement of those people they come in contact with as a result. It is, in short, contributing to the common good of society through one's work. These competences or moral habits include virtues or human qualities that are valued as positive traits and tangibly beneficial not only for ourselves but also for those around us. For example, humility leads to the acceptance of one's own limitations and mistakes; fairness means making sure that everyone receives what they are entitled to or deserve; honesty means always telling the truth; benevolence leads one to try to contribute to the common good of those around us through the decisions we make. Some other relevant moral competences or human virtues would be responsibility, loyalty, integrity, tolerance, determination, enthusiasm, and courage.

Each one of these character qualities of future professionals should be considered as part of the lifelong learning process which includes periods spent in higher education. They should be considered basic elements of a learning society, a society "in which everything affords an opportunity for learning and fulfilling one's potential" (Delors 1996, p. 36).

4.3 Contributing to the Common Good

After centuries of experience, there appears to be a consensus today that the university has a three part mission. First, the education of young people to be qualified to meet the needs and demands of society; second, the creation of new knowledge for social and economic progress, and finally, the establishment of relationships that facilitate the dissemination of the innovation that university research programs develop towards positive social change (Ranga and Etzkowitz 2013). The three part mission of the university has the same purpose and goal: the common good. Understanding this triple mission along with the search for the common good as the central theme provides a solid reference for any center of higher education. Specifically, it permits reflection on technical and moral challenges and how the right use of science can provide new strategies for new solutions. These challenges affect the scope of each area of study, and therefore, the definition of the specific competences to be developed in each subject within their individual programs.

When it comes to the competences, the learning objectives of each subject should be properly aligned with the competences of each degree program and be justified on such a basis. The process of analyzing objectives, which starts with the identification of social needs, specified in the learning objectives of each subject is not a lineal process. On the contrary, it involves much iteration to verify that the subjects are capable of instilling in students the necessary abilities to respond to social needs. The result is an unending cycle of continuing improvement based on how the needs of society also develop. A lifelong learning perspective, in this sense, means that learning can be improved with each passing day and contents, methods, and technologies used can be reviewed and expanded upon.

Therefore, there are some vital questions that educators should be asking themselves such as "how can the subject or class that I teach contribute to the more complete development of professional competences (intellectual, technical, and moral) in my students in this program?"; "how can my subject contribute to the common good?"; "what does it mean to be a graduate in the area of my discipline"?; and finally, "what should the students who take this subject know, how should they know how to put it into practice and how to do it ethically in the real world?" As mentioned previously, the question is centered upon identifying the knowledge, abilities, and learning attitudes without separating them from moral or ethical qualities and the norms of conduct that are related to the pursuit of the common good. Having answers to these questions would provide clearer guidance to instructors when defining learning objectives. These objectives are the cornerstone of good teaching and provide justification and meaning both to students in their learning and instructors in their teaching.

In addition to everything that has already been said, upon establishing objectives, instructors should take into account the background knowledge students already possess when they embark upon the subject. Only then will the challenges that are proposed be appropriate to the level of knowledge that students have. It is important to explicitly indicate that during the process described above, separations between technical and moral learning objectives should be avoided. While it is true that both constitute different dimensions, it is, however, also true that both are explored at the same time during the learning process. The key is that both dimensions need to be clearly integrated in the competences described in the degree program.

Indeed, instructors and professors should keep in mind their responsibility in developing both technical and moral skills. Typically, instructors who successfully develop technical skills are more capable of doing so with moral skills. In other words, the first contribution of an instructor to the common good is in providing good technical training. However, this would not be complete if not joined in unison with good moral training. As a final consideration concerning the purpose of the institution of the university, we would emphasize that developing intellectual, technical, and moral/ethical humanistic competences must be carried out collectively between all the instructors in each degree program and institution. When learning is not properly coordinated or when coherence does not exist between instructors and their different approaches, contributions to the common good may be negatively affected.

4.4 Developing Moral, Intellectual, and Technical Habits at the Same Time

After learning objectives and course contents are established by instructors, how do students acquire intellectual habits (knowledge), technical habits (abilities), and moral habits (virtues)? Habits, by their very nature, require the repetition of behaviors, and this is true in all three areas. Teaching methodologies should therefore provide students with the opportunity to practice those acts and behaviors desired to be developed so they can be turned into habits. Motivation in students depends on an educator's capacity to demonstrate the value and necessity of what is being taught, along with the exercises designed to reach learning objectives. Teaching based on trust assumes the premise that students understand what they are learning is good and beneficial, and that they have freely chosen to engage in the learning process.

This logic leads to teaching methods in which students exercise relevant participation. As a result, methodologies based on real or likely situations that are improvised in class are becoming more and more common. With these teaching methods that more effectively reflect future professional situations, the acquiring of intellectual, technical, and moral habits occurs more naturally through the repetition of specific actions and behaviors. Learning in any given subject, therefore, is understood as a challenge that prepares students to be able to contribute to the common good in useful ways. With this in mind, students understand and accept the effort that is required on their part to be able to participate in the learning process.

To develop habits, students need to practice the specific behaviors we want them to display in the professional world. This means that in the classroom, these behaviors should be reflected upon both individually and in groups with the assistance of instructors so that they can be improved upon. The use of case studies, role playing, and open seminars where instructors make use of the Socratic method have proven effective (Wassermann 1994; Finkel 2000; Birkenbihl 2005) in addition to supervised professional internships and other similar practicum activities that can be commented upon in class. These activities reflect real-world scenarios in which teamwork and good communication, for example, are necessary for success.

These activities effectively integrate ethical, technical, and intellectual dimensions: any physics student, for example, who knows the fundamental theory and technical dynamics of atomic energy while at the same time is trained in how it is best used, or used virtuously, is in a much better position to contribute to the common good. Any student of foreign languages, for example, who has learned to use the necessary linguistic tools to communicate at the desired professional level is also in a much better position to contribute to the common good if he or she has already practiced not only the fundamental skills of listening, reading, writing, and speaking, but also human virtues that make the ends of communication successful such as truthfulness, dialogue, tolerance, patience, and honesty. For all disciplines, both within the sciences and social sciences, it is the role of the instructor to demonstrate that both technical and human dimensions are two distinct yet inseparable realities present in all aspects of the learning experience. If it is truly the desire of educators to provide education and training that contributes to the common good, the technical and ethical dimensions, therefore, cannot be separated in the learning process.

4.5 Context, Process, and Evaluation of Moral Competence Development

Nobody questions the fact that we are social beings. Learning, therefore, is a part of our human nature which is inevitably and fundamentally social (Wenger 1998). This means that the very presence of students in the university context provides them with learning which is produced through a process which is not always explicit, but fundamentally tacit, called "socialization." As a part of this socialization at the university, instructors and professors are important figures for students. Beyond what they teach, how instructors behave provides reference, or "power of example." Whether they like it or not, instructors are an example for their students who need to perceive coherence between what they are teaching and what they practice.

When this idea is carried to the classroom, students implicitly evaluate the intellectual, technical, and moral habits that instructors propose to use in exploring and resolving problems they present in class. However, at the same time, students also evaluate if those same habits are reflected in the activities teachers carry out and in the organization and development of learning tasks. This evaluation, however, subtle and discreet, is very powerful. It requires that educational contexts be coherent. Therefore, it is important that instructors dedicate time and energy to explain and make manifest this coherence in order to avoid erroneous interpretations and perceptions. This effort is meaningful when the university community is understood and seen as an institution for the common good to which everyone should contribute, starting with the faculty.

At this point, we are conscious of the fact that getting the university to contribute harmoniously to the common good is not an easy task; however, this difficulty should not exempt educators from engaging in this reflection. What is more, a key double question arises whose urgency cannot be ignored: (1) what should be considered a coherent educational context in search of the common good? And (2) how can this be achieved in practical step-by-step terms?

The first part of the answer centers on the definition of learning objectives. They should be based on the demonstration of professional competences that contemplate the intellectual, technical, and human dimensions which are relevant and necessary so that students can willfully cooperate to contribute to the common good in today and tomorrow's world. The contents, therefore, should be appropriately adapted to the learning objectives and the number of credits awarded to the subject. Also, as mentioned previously, course contents should be appropriate for the amount of knowledge students already have so that the material offers challenges that prove neither trivial nor frustrating in their complexity.

The second part concerns systems and procedures used for evaluation. These are created after learning objectives have been established and after it has been determined how students will be led to achieve them through the learning activities introduced in the syllabus. Students, however, follow completely different systems of logic. Since it is their most basic and immediate need to pass the subject, what they learn is determined by how they think they will be evaluated.

This produces a third and final coherence factor that affects the process as a whole and completes the cycle. The learning activities that instructors propose should lead students to develop the capacity to succeed in academic evaluations following the "Three E's" Principle (Guillén 2006), that is, effectiveness (which means reaching learning objectives), efficiency (with the least effort), and ethics (with a desire for knowledge to perfect oneself and contribute to the common good). Such an approach manages academic results based on an underlying conceptual trust between students and educators. Otherwise, students will look for shortcuts, and if they find them, doubts will be cast upon the usefulness of what they are doing.

This logic, partly indebted to the principle of constructive alignment (Biggs and Tang 2007), sustains that evaluation should reflect with precision and objectivity the degree in which students have achieved learning goals. Degrees of achievement are determined in reference to learning objectives obtained through learning activities capable of creating habits (intellectual, technical, and moral) which lead students to achieve course goals effectively, efficiently, and ethically.

We would argue that an educational context that generates these teaching strategies where objectives, activities, and evaluation are aligned is coherent and generates motivation in students to learn (Ambrose et al. 2010). Moreover, when objectives, activities, and evaluation explicitly take into account the moral dimension of knowledge alongside the technical and intellectual, real and measurable humanistic training in students is easier to achieve. Humanistic training has the ultimate purpose of the betterment of all society, or, the common good.

In practical terms, educators need to slowly, thoughtfully, and responsibly plan learning programs in pursuit of the common good, and this effort needs to be contextualized within an institutional framework that shares the same objectives. Educators should reflect upon such themes beforehand, knowing that what he or she teaches and the way it is taught has direct repercussions in each and every one of their students. Furthermore, if these issues are clearly communicated to students, they would be in a much better position to understand and willingly accept the time, effort, and dedication that learning requires. Creating a context of trust and promoting the acquisition of knowledge, techniques and virtues in one's discipline is a key element in the work of an educator. From this perspective, educating acquires a moral dimension which urges instructors to be well-read and up to date on the latest research about learning, especially in the area of their disciplines. This interest is one of the qualities that characterize some of the best university educators (Bain 2004).

The process of teaching moral competence cannot be considered complete without an explicit system of evaluating results. While it is not possible to develop further this idea due to space limitations, we suggest the use of competence evaluating rubrics based on the sum of diverse criteria to evaluate different learning activities. Student writing, for example, can in such a way be made subject to the same quality levels for competence integration as the work of recognized authors. Such rubrics increase the dynamics of direct teaching as it forces students to think about the way their work will be judged before they begin to write,[2] and can be applied to other learning activities.

4.6 Conclusion

It is our position that a more holistic professional education would include moral competences (or moral virtues) in addition to intellectual and technical competences. To overcome the amorality of the framework developed for current higher education, it would be highly advisable to develop indicators for describing and evaluating moral competences. These competences, including aspects such as responsibility, integrity, honesty, equity, industriousness, loyalty, orderliness, willingness to serve, and many others, are essential professional qualifications and "to omit them would have serious consequences for future generations' ability to contribute to the sustainable development of our society" (Guillén et al. 2007, p. 418).

This chapter suggests that the concept of habit offers a view of human behavior that could help towards a fuller development of the concept of competence in general, and of "moral competence" in particular, in both the sciences and social sciences. If ethics were explicitly included as part of the learning process, the chances that more students would acquire a higher degree of moral competence would be greatly increased. But, on the other hand, if ethics is not taken explicitly into account throughout the educational process, the result is likely to produce graduates who have no notion of the rules of professional conduct, nor of the virtues they should have in order to follow those rules. On a positive note, it seems reasonable to suggest that the development of professional excellence should explicitly require continuous personal improvement, that is, the development of human excellence, and not only technical qualification.

---

[2] See https://www.teachervision.com/teaching-methods-and-management/rubrics/4522.html

References

Ambrose SA, Bridges MW, DiPietro M, Lovett MC, Norman MK (2010) How learning works: seven research-based principles for smart teaching. Wiley, San Francisco, NC

Bain K (2004) What the best college teachers do. Harvard University Press, Cambridge, MA

Bañón AJ, Guillén M, Gil I (2012) Ethics and learning organizations in the new economy. In: Juana-Espinosa S, Fernandez-Sanchez JA, Manresa-Marhuenda E, Valdes-Conca J (eds) Human resource management in the digital economy: creating synergy between competency models and information. IGI Global, Hershey, PA

Biggs J, Tang C (2007) Teaching for quality learning at university. Open University Press, Maidenhead

Birkenbihl M (2005) Train the trainer: Arbeitshandbuch für Ausbilder und Dozenten, 20th edn. Finanzbuch, München

Cardona P, García-Lombardía P (2005) How to develop leadership competencies. EUNSA, Pamplona

Delors J (1996) Learning: the treasure within. UNESCO, Paris

Finkel DL (2000) Teaching with your mouth shut. Heinemann, Portsmouth, NH

Guillén M (2006) Ethics in organizations: building trust (Spanish: Ética en las organizaciones: Construyendo confianza). Prentice-Hall (Pearson), Madrid

Guillén M, Fontrodona J, Rodríguez-Sedano A (2007) The great forgotten issue: vindicating ethics in the European qualifications framework (EQF). J Bus Ethics 74:409–423

Ranga M, Etzkowitz H (2013) Triple helix systems: an analytical framework for innovation policy and practice in the knowledge society. Ind High Educ 27(4):237–262

Wassermann S (1994) Introduction to case method teaching. A guide to the Galaxy. Teachers College Press, Columbia University, New York, NY

Wenger E (1998) Communities of practice: learning, meaning and identity. Press Syndicate of the University of Cambridge, Cambridge

Chapter 5
Applying Concept Mapping: A New Learning Strategy in Business Organisation Courses

Marta Peris-Ortiz, Diana Benito-Osorio, and Carlos Rueda-Armengot

Abstract European Higher Education Area is prompting a change in the teaching model towards the consideration of students as the main actors in the educational process. In this context, this work presents concept mapping as a useful teaching tool for promoting the development of generic and specific skills in students while also constituting a firm commitment to independent study. The technique is certainly very useful for understanding and framing strategies, theories and concepts and provides visualisation of typical connections between different concepts, interrelations among strategies, analysis of the consequences of business decision-making and so on among others.

Concept mapping was used by 355 students on the Principles of Business Organisation course in the second year of the Industrial Technologies Engineering degree course. As a general outcome of the study, marks in the subject show considerable improvement in all the groups.

5.1 Introduction

Universities are currently experiencing a period of change and restructuring into what is known as the European Higher Education Area (EHEA). EHEA represents a process of educational reform based on three types of transformations: structural,

---

M. Peris-Ortiz (✉) • C. Rueda-Armengot
Departamento de Organización de Empresas, Universitat Politècnica de València,
Camino de Vera, 46022 Valencia, Spain
e-mail: mperis@doe.upv.es; crueda@doe.upv.es

D. Benito-Osorio
Departamento de Economía de la Empresa (Administración, Dirección y Organización),
Rey Juan Carlos University, Paseo de los artilleros, Madrid, Spain
e-mail: diana.benito@urjc.es

curricular and organisational. The integration of Spanish universities in this new EHEA is bringing conceptual and methodological changes not just to the structure of university education, but also to the teaching–learning processes and the conditions under which they take place. This work focuses on organisational changes.

EHEA is prompting a change in the teaching model towards the consideration of students as the main actors in the educational process. This change requires new teaching strategies where students are asked to resolve problems with tools provided by the teacher. In this context, this work presents concept mapping as a useful teaching tool for promoting the development of generic and specific skills in students while also constituting a firm commitment to independent study. We address the usefulness and content of this approach in relation to the various competences it is intended to promote in the Principles of Business Organisation course.

Universities in Spain and Europe are currently undergoing a period of change and restructuring. As ANECA indicated in the 2005 draft White Paper on Pedagogy and Social Education Degrees before 2010, a process of convergence of the Spanish university system with what is known as the EHEA began. This process is bringing a series of transformations in the structure and operation of all university courses (ANECA 2005a, b).

This educational reform, like others, is based on three types of transformations in the university system: structural, curricular and organisational. Structural changes affect the division and duration of educational stages, curricular changes affect the definition, design and development of the curriculum and organisational changes affect the conditions in which learning and teaching take place and therefore depend directly on the institutions involved (Mateo 2000). In this work we focus on organisational changes. In particular, the inclusion of generic and specific competences in teaching requires academic leaders who are effective in the knowledge society and use innovation and creativity to promote the development of appropriate competences in EHEA.

The integration of Spanish universities in this new EHEA is therefore bringing both conceptual and methodological changes not just to the structure of university studies but also to the teaching and learning processes and the conditions under which they take place (e.g. ANECA 2005a, b; González and Wagenar 2003; Pagani 2002; R.D. 1125/2003; R.D. 55/2005; R.D. 56/2005). The EHEA is transforming the teaching model towards consideration of students as the protagonists of the educational process. This approach requires the application of new teaching strategies in which students are able to resolve the problems put before them using the tools the teacher provides. In this new scenario, training students in competences have become a key issue that requires university teachers to have new teaching tools at their disposal. These new teaching strategies will affect the quality of education and involve the use of a broad range of techniques. One such technique is the production and development of concept maps. Concept mapping has become a widely used educational tool around the globe (Hwang et al. 2013).

Concept mapping is a constructivist learning strategy that delivers significant learning experiences by relating concepts. Its characteristics are simplification, hierarchisation and visual impact. People of all ages and all domains of knowledge have been using concept mapping for many years as a tool to express their understanding about a topic (Cañas et al. 2013). In this context, this work aims to present the concept mapping as a useful didactic tool for promoting the development of generic and specific competences in students while also constituting a firm commitment to independent study. We address the utility and content of concept mapping in relation to various competences being sought through its use in a course on the Principles of Business Organisation.

The planning of the activities requires consideration of the intended aims and definition of the most appropriate tasks. It is important to have a varied methodology and there are different perspectives for classifying methodological strategies (Fandos Garrido and González Soto 2005). Bearing in mind the criteria suggested by Esteban (2003), we classify teaching strategies into associative, productive and organisational strategies.

Organisational strategies consist in explicitly establishing internal relations between the elements in learning materials and students' prior knowledge. Prior knowledge operates in two ways: first, because it depends on what that prior knowledge is (quantity and quality) and thus students' ability to produce more or less complex materials and second, because the cognitive structure resulting from the new knowledge will modify the organisation of the existing knowledge. Organisational strategies are often classified as follows: the construction of knowledge networks (networking); higher level structures (covariation, comparison, collection, description and response) each of which implies a specific cognitive technique; Gowin's V mapping strategies and, of course, concept mapping. It seems very appropriate to use an organisational strategy in a course on business organisation.

5.2 Concept Mapping as Learning Methodology in Business Organisation

5.2.1 The Concept Mapping Concept

First proposed by Novak and Gowin (1984), a concept map is a graphical tool for organising and representing knowledge (Ruiz-Primo et al. 1997). The use of concept mapping in teaching business organisation is well documented. More generally, in education, concept maps have been shown to be useful as a tool for teachers to assess students' understanding, whether at the beginning, during, or at the end of a course (Novak and Cañas 2004). Teachers often support their lectures with diagrams adapted to the particular topic they are teaching to help students understand the theoretical content. The novelty of this method, however, lies in the production of these diagrams in order to perfect the teaching technique; that is, concept mapping by expert teachers who want to generalise the use of these diagrams for teaching purposes, because of their confidence in the performance of these teaching tools.

Concept mapping is defined as the graphic or symbolic representation (descriptive and systematised) of concepts and figures to reflect essential connections and interrelations and which help to reveal their nature and/or basic operation. That is, visual networks and concept mapping to continue with the terminology used by Novak (1998) are forms of graphic representation that reinforce cognitive and learning processes by concepts presented visually and ordered in a linear hierarchical manner according to their own explanatory valence. The aim is simply to represent significant relationships between ideas, words and visual features so that students activate their reasoning by interacting with the nodules on each graph. The applications of concept mapping, however, have increased in number, and this technique now appears extensively as an assessment tool. In fact, the literature is abundant with studies on the use of concept maps for assessment and on the assessment of concept maps (Cañas et al. 2013).

Conceptual mapping favours the development of important competences such as the ability to summarise and analyse, and is particularly well suited to teaching the discipline of business organisation. As Alemán Páez (2009) points out the structure of concept maps initiates the processes of interpretation, integration and annunciation of propositions. They clarify information density and the ability to summarise. By facilitating rereading, they are also a powerful mnemonic and retention instrument, containing a range of words and ideas that provide students with the opportunity to gradually enrich their conceptual and technical vocabulary on the subject. However, the creation of concept maps also requires teachers to make the effort to summarise, systematise contents and their interrelationships, make synoptic tables and condense information.

5.2.2 How to Produce a Concept Map

According to proposals from Novak and Gowin (1984), Ontoria (1993), Pérez Cabaní (1995) and González García (1992), the production of a concept map involves the following steps:

1. Identify the key concepts of the content to be ordered on the map. These concepts should be put in a list.
2. Place the main or more general concept at the top of the map and gradually join it to other concepts according to their level of generalisation and specificity. All concepts should be written in capital letters.
3. Connect the concepts with the link words which should be written in small letters in the middle of two lines that indicate the direction of the proposition.
4. Examples can be included at the bottom of the map, under the corresponding concepts.
5. After observing all the linear concepts, cross-linked relations can be observed.

Considering the classroom, if the intention is to produce a concept map at group level it is always better to propose it as a complete work at individual level and then reach a commonly agreed map by analysing each map and the justifications given by the authors. The process is slower but reflects group work better.

The main elements in a concept map are:

- Concept: is an event or object which is regularly denominated by name or label (Novak and Gowin 1984). The concept can be considered as the word used to designate a certain image of an object or an event that occurs in individuals' minds, there are concepts which define concrete elements (house, desk) and others that define abstract notions which we cannot touch but are a reality (democracy, state). Concepts are included in boxes or circles and the relations between them are explained by lines joining the respective boxes.
- Connectors: are prepositions, conjunctions, adverbs and in general all words that are not a concept and are used to relate concepts and thus assemble a "proposition" for example: for, by, where, how, among others. Link words, together with concepts, permit the construction of phrases or sentences with a logical significance and help to find the connection between concepts.
- Proposition: a proposition is a phrase about a certain object or event in the universe which occurs naturally or artificially. Propositions contain two or more concepts connected with other words which form a coherent sentence. They are usually called "semantic units".
- Link lines and arrows: in the conceptual maps conventionally arrows are not used because the relationship between concepts is specified by link words and lines are used to join concepts. Novak and Gowin (1984) reserve the use of arrows only in the case where the relationship in question is not one of subordination between concepts and therefore they can be used to represent a cross-linked relationship between concepts from one section of the map and those from the other side of the conceptual "tree". The arrow indicates that there is no subordinate relationship.

5.2.3 Concept Mapping as a Teaching and Learning Tool

Advances in computer interface technology have led to even more alternatives for using concept maps in teaching and learning (Hwang et al. 2013). Concept mapping as a teaching resource in higher education presents a wide range of possibilities: teachers can use the maps as a way of presenting information; students can create maps for a subject, concept maps can organise the design of materials for learning, relating knowledge, etc. (Cañas et al. 2000). Of all these, here it is of interest to examine concept maps as integrators of the teaching and learning strategy, that is, as a tool for students to retain information on a topic, integrate and organise it with the information they already have.

Thus concept mapping is particularly effective in the teaching of business although its effectiveness depends on how well the teacher masters the technique. It is of course very useful for explaining, understanding and framing strategies, decision-making processes, theories, concepts, etc. in the right place in the huge context of business organisation it provides added value for understanding business economics as a scientific discipline. In this same vein, the principle of unity that governs strategic business management increases the utility and use of this type of teaching materials which provide visualisation of typical connections between different concepts and the interrelation between strategies and analysis of the consequences of business decision-making.

The visual impact of the diagram on students is undeniable, Hudson and Buckley (2004) simplifying complexity through a basic graphic structure facilitates assimilation of more difficult concepts (they are made visible just by looking at the diagram), this approach promotes the acquisition of particularly complicated and difficult content, recognition of the main connections in each figure or category permitting retention of the key factors in their operation and finally the main ideas are exhaustively refined in detail. For all these reasons, teachers can use maps during their classes, motivating interiorisation of verbal explanations and student participation in relation to the contents in the diagram.

5.3 Applied to the Field of Business Organisation

The experiment was applied to 355 students of the principles of business organisation course in the second year of the Engineering degree in Industrial Technology at the Advanced School of Industrial Engineering at Polytechnic University of Valencia. A considerable improvement was observed in all the groups' marks in the subject.

5.3.1 Methodology Planning the Use of Conceptual Mapping with Students

Conceptual mapping was used as follows:

A practical session was prepared at the start of the course with the object of presenting students with the tool for producing conceptual maps. In terms of learning attitudes and the degree of acceptance of concept mapping in learning, students are more positive about the two-touch technology-based interaction modes than they were about the traditional paper-and-pencil mode (Hwang et al. 2013). In this case, the tool was Visual Understanding Environment v.3.1 (http://vue.tufts.edu/) (e.g. Kumar and Saigal 2005; Yao and Gu 2013), chosen because it is easy to use and, above all, it is freeware. Other similar tools such as Cmaptools also exist, however (e.g. Novak and Cañas 2004; Utari et al. 2013).

After this session, students were randomly organised into groups. This method was chosen to avoid established vices in working in groups of people who knew each other well while also ensuring that they used social networks and the Poliformat platform to carry out the work.

Similarly, the students were told that the conceptual map produced by each group would be presented and commented on with the teacher by each member of the group. Interviews were chosen as the form for evaluating this practical work as it was the most appropriate way of showing the degree of integration of knowledge in students, for presenting complex thought and ultimately, for resolving conceptual problems. The interview was unstructured with a constant objective while the questions were adapted according to the way the interview evolved.

Finally, it is planned to create a repository of these maps for future students to consult.

Students were expected to be able to:

- Explain the significance of the key concepts reflected on their maps.
- Defend the absence of key concepts.
- Reorganise connections between different key concept on the map.
- Describe and defend their proposed map.
- Relate it to other knowledge of their own.
- Defend proposals for ordering knowledge rejected by that group.

Given the characteristics of the course used in the experiment, it was not possible to establish a control group to determine the significance of the final marks obtained by each student and therefore the results can only be assessed qualitatively.

In contrast to recommendations from different fields since the introduction of degree studies, students were under no obligation to attend class.

However, teachers of the subject agreed that there was an average regular attendance of 95 % over the first ten sessions of class, and various students dropped out half way through the course in the final sessions This represents a notable increase in attendance in relation to the management course which preceded the principles of business organisation course.

5.3.2 Results

Considered globally, the results of the experiment can be said, in principle, to be positive concept maps have proven to be powerful tools for organising and integrating knowledge.

Students have been more interested in the development of the subject, the questions and reasoning they put forward during class discussions were, in general, qualitatively better than those in other courses and in general the level of satisfaction with the subject is high in all groups. These results are in line with many previous studies that have shown that concept mapping strategies may improve students' academic achievement (Erdogan 2009; Hwang et al. 2011; Lim et al. 2009).

As regards teaching the classes, the teachers found the experience to be "interesting", "valid" and "enriching", which suggests that to a certain extent teachers of the subject have also been enriched by class discussions and reflections. Teachers' level of satisfaction with the global results for the subject was high, with 100 % of students sitting the exam and a 92 % pass rate in the final marks. In addition, researchers have also indicated that a potential way for educators to conduct concept map-based instruction is to use computerised tools in place of traditional paper-based approaches (Kim and Olaciregui 2008).

5.4 Conclusions

From the experiment applied to the principles of business organisation course, it can be concluded that at least in analytical type subjects where the aim is to develop in particular conceptual aptitudes that permit identification of important information or knowledge and then integrate it rather than interiorising a set of solutions or pre-established formula, abandoning the lecture is, in principle, positive. However, the true challenge is to get students to prepare the session and of course, to participate.

Secondly, we can conclude that at least from a qualitative assessment, concept mapping is a good tool for integrating concepts and developing knowledge. However, improvements can be made to the way it has been implemented in the subject According to the teachers rather than developing a complete conceptual map per group perhaps partial concept maps should be made to then discuss how to integrate them in a global map, created not per group but per class.

Acknowledgements Research reported in this paper was supported by Universitat Politècnica de València (Spain) Project PIME A07-13.

References

Alemán Páez F (2009) Materiales Prácticos y Recursos Didácticos para la Enseñanza del Derecho del Trabajo y las Políticas Sociolaborales (Adaptado al EEES). Tecnos, Madrid

ANECA (2005a) Libro Blanco del Título de Grado en Pedagogía y Educación Social I. Agencia Nacional de Evaluación de la Calidad y Acreditación, Madrid. http://www.aneca.es/var/media/150392/libroblanco_pedagogia1_0305.pdf

ANECA (2005b) Libro Blanco del Título de Grado en Pedagogía y Educación Social II. Agencia Nacional de Evaluación de la Calidad y Acreditación, Madrid. http://www.aneca.es/var/media/150392/libroblanco_pedagogia1_0305.pdf

Cañas AJ, Ford KM, Coffey J, Reichherzer T, Carff R, Shamma D, Breedy M (2000) Herramientas para Construir y Compartir Modelos de Conocimiento basados en Mapas Conceptuales. Rev Inform Educ Colombia 13(2):145–158

Cañas JA, Bunch L, Novak JD, Reiska P (2013) Cmapanalysis: an extensible concept map analysis tool. J Educ Teach Train 4(1):36–46

Erdogan Y (2009) Paper-based and computer-based concept mappings: the effects on computer achievement, computer anxiety and computer attitude. Br J Educ Technol 40:821–836

Esteban M (2003) Las estrategias de aprendizaje en el entorno de la Educación a Distancia (EaD). Consideraciones para la reflexión y el debate. Introducción al estudio de las estrategias y estilos de aprendizaje [en línea]. Rev Educ Distancia 7:1–4. http://www.um.es/ead/red/7/estrategias.pdf

Fandos Garrido M, González Soto AP (2005) Estrategias de aprendizaje ante las nuevas posibilidades educativas de las TIC [en línea]. http://www.formatex.org/micte2005/227.pdf

González García G (1992) Los mapas conceptuales de J D Novak como instrumentos para la investigación didáctica de las ciencias experimentales. Enseñ Cien 10(2):148–158

González J, Wagenar R (2003) Tuning educational structures in Europe. Universidad de Deusto, Bilbao

Hudson JN, Buckley P (2004) An evaluation of case-based teaching: evidence for continuing benefit and a realization of aims. Adv Physiol Educ 28:15–22

Hwang G-J, Shi Y-R, Chu H-C (2011) A concept map approach to developing collaborative mindtools for context-aware ubiquitous learning. Br J Educ Technol 42:778–789

Hwang G-J, Wu C-H, Kuo F-R (2013) Effects of touch technology-based concept mapping on students' learning attitudes and perceptions. Educ Technol Soc 16(3):274–285

Kim P, Olaciregui C (2008) The effects of a concept map-based information display in an electronic portfolio system on information processing and retention in a fifth-grade science class covering the Earth's atmosphere. Br J Educ Technol 39:700–714

Kumar A, Saigal R (2005) Visual understanding environment. In Proceedings of the fifth ACM/IEEE-CS joint conference on digital libraries (JCDL'05), IEEE, pp 413–413

Lim KY, Lee HW, Grabowski B (2009) Does concept-mapping strategy work for everyone? The levels of generativity and learners' self-regulated learning skills. Br J Educ Technol 40:606–618

Mateo J (2000) La evaluación educativa, su práctica y otras metáforas. Universidad de Barcelona-Horsori, Barcelona

Novak JD (1998) Learning, creating, and using knowledge: concept maps as facilitative tools for schools and corporations. Lawrence Erlbaum, Mahwah, NJ

Novak JD, Cañas AJ (2004) Building on constructivist ideas and Cmaptools to create a new model for education. In: Cañas AJ, Novak JD, González FM (eds) Concept maps: theory, methodology, technology. Proceedings of the first international conference on concept mapping. Universidad Pública de Navarra, Pamplona, Spain

Novak JD, Gowin DB (1984) Learning how to learn. Cambridge University Press, Cambridge

Ontoria A (1993) Mapas conceptuales. Una Técnica para Aprender. Editorial Narcea, Madrid

Pagani R (2002) El crédito europeo y el Sistema Educativo Español. Edición electrónica. http://www.um.es

Pérez Cabaní ML (1995) Los mapas conceptuales. Cuad Pedagog 237:16–21

Ruiz-Primo MA, Shavelson RJ, Schultz SE (1997) On the validity of concept map-base assessment interpretations: an experiment testing the assumption of hierarchical concept maps in science. National Center for Research on Evaluation, Standards, and Student Testing (CRESST), Center for the Study of Evaluation (CSE), Graduate School of Education & Information Studies, University of California, Los Angeles

Utari SS, Alfiani A, Feranie S, Aviyanti L, Sari IM, Hasanah L (2013) Application of learning cycle 5e model aided Cmaptools-based media prototype to improve student cognitive learning outcomes. Appl Phys Res 5(4):69–76

Yao J, Gu M (2013) Conceptology: using concept map for knowledge representation and ontology construction. J Netw 8(8):1708–1712

Chapter 6
Pedagogical Innovation in Higher Education: Teachers' Perceptions

Cristina Mesquita, Rui Pedro Lopes, José Álvarez García, and María de la Cruz del Río Rama

Abstract The regulation changes we have been witnessing in Portugal in the last 5 or 6 years have been introducing new degrees, new diplomas and new audiences in higher education. The Technological Specialization Courses where created in this context, providing a more vocational and technical post-secondary training.

These courses are of the responsibility of Higher Education Institutions (HEIs) and their faculty, presenting a whole new set of pedagogical difficulties and challenges.

In this chapter we present a study, performed in the Polytechnic Institute of Bragança, a public HEI, that aims to understand the perceptions and expectations of teachers in relation to this kind of courses in terms of students, curriculum, pedagogical methodologies, and satisfaction. The following pages describe the theoretical background, the study methodology, and the result analysis, focusing on the pedagogical changes and strategies towards the improvement of teachers' professional skills and students' intellectual and ethical development.

C. Mesquita
Department of Social Sciences, Polytechnic Institute of Bragança,
Campus St. Apolónia, 5301 Bragança, Portugal
e-mail: cmmgp@ipb.pt

R.P. Lopes
Department of Informatics and Communications, Polytechnic Institute of Bragança,
Campus St. Apolónia, 5301 Bragança, Portugal
e-mail: rlopes@ipb.pt

J.Á. García (✉)
Departamento de Finanzas y contabilidad, University of Extremadura,
Av. Universidad, 10003 Cáceres, Spain
e-mail: pepealvarez@unex.es

M. de la Cruz del Río Rama
Departamento de Organización de Empresas y Márketing, Unicersity of Vigo,
As Lagoas. s/n 32004, Vigo, Spain
e-mail: delrio@uvigo.es

6.1 Introduction

The qualification of human capital is fundamental to ensure competitiveness, personal and cultural development and social cohesion enhancement. Education policies in Portugal have been encouraging the access to higher education to new audiences, by creating new opportunities to untraditional students, such as the "Greater than 23 Years Old" or the Technological Specialization Courses (CET). These were created to counter the high dropout rates at secondary level, allowing early entrance in the labor market by specialized youth as well as the study progression at higher education level (Legislative Degree n. 88/2006, of the 23th of May). They also provide an opportunity to students, having failed secondary education, to integrate either academic or professional life trough a Technological Specialization Diploma.

On the other hand, they also represent a possibility for Higher Education Institutions (HEIs), in particular the ones located in the interior of the country, to compensate the decreasing number of students that have been occurring in the last years, mainly for demographic reasons.

The increasing number of this kind of students has been presenting a challenge, both organizational and pedagogical. It is fundamental to understand the characteristics of this audience as well as the perceptions and expectations of teachers, to allow better decision making about training strategies and teachers' profile. In this context, the reflection described in this chapter is centered on the teachers, analyzing what they think the best pedagogical approaches are, the students' characteristics, the best training model, and teachers' performance and satisfaction.

6.2 New Challenges in Higher Education

The constant transformations that have been occurring, as a result of the economic, political, and cultural globalization, highlights the need to adapt training to new specialization requirements and to the permanent requalification of people.

It is clear that, in this context, the human capital qualification is a fundamental factor to the promotion of competitiveness, personal and cultural development as well as for social cohesion. The European goals set for 2020 demand, for higher education in Portugal, an increased effort towards matching the European parameters (Bessa et al. 2013).

According to these goals, the education policies in Portugal have been encouraging the integration of new audiences in higher education, creating new opportunities to untraditional candidates, such as the "Greater than 23 years old," or broadening the training offer through the CET.

The increasing number of students with theses characteristics represents a challenge, both organizational and pedagogical, to the institutions that receive them. Moreover, the Bologna paradigm requires some reflection about the specificities of these audiences, as well as the best training strategies and the most adequate teacher profile to support this kind of students. HEI should assume new training strategies that can respond adequately to increasingly heterogeneous students (Pedrosa 2001).

Teachers are required to hold solid scientific experience and training as well as academic expertize, towards the creation of knowledge. However, this new reality also requires the development of relational and pedagogical skills. This poses some challenges, derived from the implementation of the Bologna Process paradigm and from the necessity of innovating in the pedagogical area in higher education training.

6.2.1 The Bologna Process and Inherent Challenges

As previously referred, the Bologna Declaration has introduced important modifications in the structure and pedagogical design of higher education courses, including the requirements of the training process adequacy to the labor market needs and the reorganization of the higher education training cycles to increase the flexibility of the overall academic process (Union Europea 2010).

The restructuring of courses according to these principles is instantiated in a European higher education area of research and innovation, supporting student mobility and promotion of employability, as well as in the evolution of the training paradigm, comprising the different phases in the adult life and the adaptation to the evolution of knowledge and other individual and collective interests.

However, although the Bologna Process values the student-centered learning, the pedagogical model of knowledge acquisition has been prevailing. The organizational logic and conceptualization has been unable to deconstruct traditional learning models, since it is supported by the process-product paradigm in which the essential knowledge is inventoried and delivered during the training period. This logic is conceived "within a tylerian logic of curricular development, previously defining knowledge, know-how and attitudes necessary to the profession" (Estrela 2002).

The training process is based on an asymmetry between the roles of the teacher and the student, too much centered in the information over the process of knowledge production. In this context, the reconstruction and reintegration of knowledge is seldom perceived (Canário 2002).

The way the Bologna Declaration was implemented in the several HEI indicates the continuity of previous pedagogical models, following a traditional academic approach. It was influenced by an external process, resulting from the guidelines enforced by the Science and Higher Education Ministry, without a real involvement of teachers (Teodoro 2005). Courses were organized in three cycles, starting with a 3-year, broad scope degree. The second cycle corresponds to the master degree, with 2-year duration. The last, 4-year long, cycle corresponds to doctoral studies. Moreover, the guidelines also value the autonomous working hours by the students, which resulted in the reduction of contact hours.

However, the established academic culture in higher education also influenced the course structure to follow a sectoral perspective (Hargreaves 1998). The external pressure should promote the discussion around the required changes. However, they should really come from within, to cope with the strong and meaningfulness training of students (Campos 2002):

> although the ultimate mission of higher education is to build culture, we tend to pose a comprehensible resistance to cultural changes relative to our own practices. By not being actors of such changes, we oppose to simply accept them, reinforcing the social conviction of the impossibility of self-training in higher education. The secret is in the conditions required to take us from a first opposing attitude (conservative) to the involvement in the construction of new practices (p. 91).

Following the legal diplomas, the structure of subjects gives relevance to the acquisition-centered model. The "organizational configuration that supports and is supported by the prevailing subject supremacy and the exclusion of 'more practical' mentalities [...] narrow the organizational learning and the educational change and endures and expresses the conflicts and divisions" (Hargreaves 1998).

In this context, the debate between ideas established in the confrontation of two training models appeared: the academic (centered in the acquisition of basic competences, necessary to the exercise of teaching) and the professional (valuing the in context training and the continuous development of the subject).

The construction of common languages and meanings between actors and the definition of projects for a new direction of training would claim time, sharing, collaborative culture, and creativity. The professional development is, in this context, incompatible with the simple implementation of curricular directives.

Moreover, the curricular structure often reveals inter-department tensions and the survivability within the institution, enduring the sectoral training model. The legal and technological tendency appears to prevail, undervaluing the pedagogical component and the curricular articulation that Bologna claims.

6.2.2 The Pedagogical Implications in the New Paradigm

HEI have three primary missions: education, research, and cooperation (Cachapuz 2001). While in different weights and strategic importance, most institutions try to cope with these missions to contribute for population education at high level, scientific and technological advances, and economic and social development. These threefold approaches to professional development introduce some stress within teachers, demanding a constant balance between them.

This reality becomes even more complex when teachers, used to share knowledge, know-how and research topics, do not demonstrate the same sharing culture in relation to the subjects they teach (Shulman 1993). Moreover, the overrating of scientific activity over teaching also has the consequence that the professional prestige will result essentially from the investment in research, subordinating the teaching activity.

The changes that the Bologna Declaration brings, as referred above, is centered on self-learning instead of knowledge transmission, requiring a different way to look at higher education. Teachers should adopt pedagogical models that are supported in an ethical dimension, and overall respect by who is learning and how they are learning (Nóvoa 2002).

Teachers should adopt pedagogical strategies and methodologies more adequate to their students. They should also reflect on the contribute that the subjects they are teaching brings to the future professionals and how they articulate with other subjects, as well as all the associated resources that support the pedagogical and international dynamics within the classroom (Dill 2003).

Along with a solid scientific knowledge, teachers should also have sufficient pedagogical know-how to help students build meaning about the scientific knowledge and its practical relevance. This pedagogical knowledge of content implies the necessary articulation between what one knows and how it is communicated to who is learning and will use in the future (Shulman 1993).

In this perspective, HEI have also the responsibility to provide adequate environment to pedagogical development of the teaching staff. This also requires that each teacher will assume the role of researcher of his own practice (Zeichner 1993), focusing on the teacher but based on the cooperation between colleagues (Garcia 1999).

Some experiences performed with higher education teachers emphasize that some pedagogical strategies, such as the involvement of teachers in their own pedagogical training (Pinto 2008), tutorial supervision, and project-based learning, contribute to the integration and success of students (Simão et al. 2008). These experiences highlight the relevance of a "culture of good practice" within the institutions, which values the pedagogical activity.

The importance of the pedagogical training of teachers in higher education, as described above, requires an insight on how teachers perceive their own performance in a new student-centered paradigm. It is also important to build an adequate profile to accommodate the new audiences in higher education. To assess this, we conducted a study in a public HEI, focusing on the specific case of the Technological Specialization Courses.

6.3 Analysis

When this study was made, the Polytechnic Institute of Bragança had 33 CET, distributed in seven scientific areas (Fig. 6.1). The subjects were lectured by 230 teachers, among the institute's five schools.

We followed a quantitative research methodology where data was collected through an online questionnaire and consequent statistical analysis. The questionnaire was distributed to the 230 teachers, of which we obtained 87 responses. Assuming a degree of confidence of 95 %, considering that the percentage of responses is of 38 %, the interval of confidence is between 1.6 and 8 %, which allows us to conclude that the obtained number of responses is sufficient to a precise analysis and meaningful results.

Fig. 6.1 Number of CET in the IPB

Table 6.1 Category and degree of teachers

	Assistant	Auxiliary professors	Full professors
Ph.D.	2	27	5
Specialist	1	2	0
M.Sc.	27	3	0
Degree	19	1	0

The questionnaire comprises 16 items, structured in five dimensions:

1. Teachers' characterization.
2. The integration of the CET in the higher education.
3. The training model (curriculum, practical training, methodology and operation).
4. Teachers' performance (methodology, evaluation, and satisfaction).
5. Students' characterization.

The data analysis was performed with the general-purpose statistical software STATA, version 12.1.

6.3.1 Characterization of Respondents

Of all the respondents, 51.2 % are male and 48.8 % are female (balanced relation among gender). Teachers' age is between 20 and 50 years old, with 44.8 % in the range 31–40 and 37.9 % between 41 and 50.

Among the 87 teachers, 23 have a partial contract and 64 have an integral contract. In terms of category, five are full professors, 33 are auxiliary professors, and 49 are assistant professors (56 %). Moreover, 34 hold a Ph.D., three are specialists, and 30 have an M.Sc. (Table 6.1).

6.3.2 Integration of CET in the HEI

The CET are post-secondary technological courses, focusing on practical subjects and training. Although these are not considered as higher education courses in the traditional sense, the law specifically delegates to the HEI the responsibility for them. The scientific and pedagogical requirements are different from B.Sc. and M.Sc. courses, which require some adaptation from the organization as well as from the teachers.

Hereupon, the teachers' perception regarding the integration of the CET in the HEI is relevant to assess their concern and availability to adapt learning experiences and pedagogical approach to the specificities of these courses.

The integration of CET in the HEI section of the survey comprises six questions, using a five-point Likert scale (1. Totally disagree; 2. Disagree; 3. Don't agree nor disagree; 4. Agree; 5. Totally agree). The answers were grouped in two groups: the first containing all the 1 and 2 answers and the other with all the 4 and 5 answers. The intermediate level (3) was not considered in the analysis.

The mission of the CET is to specialize students in a profession, in a short training cycle. 71.3 % of the teachers agree that this mission is adequate and perfectly in the scope of the HEI (74.7 %). They, further support that the HEI are the best prepared to assume this responsibility (62.2 %).

Teachers also believe that high academic degrees are important (55.2 %). However, 42.5 % also believe that the B.Sc. degree is enough and 28.7 % say that the degree is not important.

6.3.3 Training Model

The training model of the CET was assessed in a four group section of the survey, using the same approach as the above. The four groups are:

1. Curriculum—the relation of the subjects with the B.Sc., the complexity and extension of the content, practice and theory components, and student autonomy.
2. Practical training—further details regarding the theory and practice as well as the articulation between the internship organization and the university.
3. Methodology—the learning experiences and pedagogical approaches.
4. Operation—Infrastructures, classroom resources, hour distribution, and class dimension.

The curriculum is organized, in broad terms, in theory and practice. Teachers believe that there is an adequate balance between both components (72.1 %) and that the time for practice component is adequate (57.6 %).

However, although believing that students learn better when confronting theory with the actions developed through practice (95.3 %) and that the reflection should include all the actors in the training process (86.1 %), teachers continue to overvalue theory over practice (88.5 %). Moreover, although teachers value active participation, 52.9 % say that the transmissive approach does not reduce the possibilities for students' participation.

6.3.4 Teachers' Performance

The performance of teachers' section of the survey is structured in three groups, namely the pedagogical methodology, the evaluation of students, and the teacher's satisfaction. The questions for each group use a five-point Likert scale, and the answers were groups as above.

As expected, 90.8 % of the teachers consider that the CET require a methodology centered on the student. However, 65.1 % acknowledge that they are using the expository method, considering that this is the most adequate method for this kind of training.

When questioned about the pedagogical methodologies, 83.1 % feel comfortable in using different pedagogical methodologies and 63.4 % say that no further pedagogical training is necessary. Teachers with higher academic degree do recognize that further pedagogical training would be beneficial (with 95 % statistical confidence).

Teachers are globally satisfied with their performance in lecturing the CET (78.8 %). However, teachers with a Ph.D. are less satisfied (3.6 average) than the B.Sc. and M.Sc. (4.2 average), with a statistical confidence of 99.9 %.

6.3.5 Characterization of Students

The student characterization by the teachers is performed through seven questions, using a five-point Likert scale. Just like above, the answers were grouped in two groups: the first containing all the 1 and 2 answers and the other with all the 4 and 5 answers. The intermediate level (3) was not considered in the analysis.

Teachers recognize that students do not have study habits (63.5 %), only studying for the exams (65.9 %). On the other hand, teachers also recognize that it is easy to motivate students with practical and hands-on work (65.9 %) and that they demonstrate interest during classes (58.3 %).

51.8 % of the teachers also consider that students are not prepared to the CET demands and complexity, with particular incidence in technological areas (99.1 % statistical relevance). However, they do not conduct diagnostic evaluation (56.5 %).

6.4 Conclusions

The accommodation of students with untraditional profiles in higher education, in the student-centered learning paradigm defined by the Bologna Declaration requires a concrete adequacy of pedagogical models and learning experiences. To assess the perception of teachers about their own performance as well as to assess how they feel about the students profile and integration, we conducted a study comprising 230 teachers.

The results suggest that teachers consider that the CET is perfectly adequate and fall into the missions of the HEI, preparing students to the exercise of a profession. They also believe that teachers hold adequate academic degree for lecturing them.

The CET training model is well structured and balanced between theoretical and practice. However, data reveals that teachers, in fact, use an applicationist perspective of theory on professional practice.

Teachers consider themselves informed of the several pedagogical strategies and techniques and they feel comfortable in how they develop their own pedagogical action, not being motivated for further pedagogical training. However, they also say that they are using almost exclusively, transmissive techniques. These may be explained because they are mostly interested in investing in the research area, since this is more probable to foster academic career, appealing mostly to younger teachers. The transmissive methods are typical in higher education, and its replication is natural, because of the lack of pedagogical training.

Higher academic degrees reveal less satisfaction with their own work. This perception probably arises from the fact that they feel pedagogically unprepared to lecture this audience or from the feeling that high academic degree is not valued in this context.

The perception about study habits, previous knowledge, and needs of students changes along the process. This is supported by the fact that there is no diagnostic evaluation, no consideration about students' abilities in planning the material and learning experiences, nor the use of methodologies that value the participative construction of knowledge.

In summary, the study reveals the need to develop in context training, to help teachers build a more realistic perspective of this new audience profile, in the sense to adequate the teaching/learning process to the demands of a specialized training and the appreciation of the active participation of students in their own process of personal empowerment. Institutions should be alert to the teachers' pedagogical needs, discussing and developing projects to promote the professional development of the teaching staff thus contributing to an installed "culture of good practice."

References

Bessa D, Estanque E, Villaverde Cabral M, Pita Barros P (2013) Comentários ao Estudo—25 Anos de Portugal Europeu. Technical report, Fundação Francisco Manuel dos Santos. URL: http://www.ffms.pt/estudo/18/25-anos-de-portugal-europeu

Cachapuz A (2001) Em defesa do aperfeiçoamento pedagógico dos docentes do ensino superior. Edições Colibri, Lisboa

Campos BP (2002) Formação profissional de professores no ensino superior. Porto Editora, Porto

Canário R (2002) Formação inicial de professores: que futuro (s)? Síntese dos relatórios de avaliação dos cursos para o 3º ciclo do ensino básico e ensino secundário. Estudos sobre a situação da formação inicial de professores. Porto Editora, Porto

Dill D (2003) An institutional perspective on higher education policy: the case of academic quality assurance. In: Smart J (ed) Higher education: handbook of theory and research. Springer, The Netherlands, pp 669–699

Estrela MT (2002) Modelos de formação de professores e seus pressupostos conceptuais. Rev Educ 11(1):17–29

Garcia CM (1999) Formação de professores. Para uma mudança educativa. Porto Editora, Porto

Hargreaves A (1998) Os professores em tempos de mudança: o trabalho e a cultura dos professores na idade pós-moderna. McGraw-Hill de Portugal, Alfragide

Nóvoa A (2002) Formação de professores e trabalho pedagógico. Educa, Lisboa

Pedrosa J (2001) A formação pedagógica dos professores do ensino superior. Edições Colibri, Lisboa

Pinto PR (2008) Formação pedagógica no ensino superior. Sísifo Rev Ciên Educ 7:111–124

Shulman LS (1993) Forum: teaching as community property: putting an end to pedagogical solitude. Change 25(6):6–7

Simão AMV, Flores M, Fernandes S, Figueira C (2008) Tutoria no ensino superior: concepções e práticas. Sísifo Rev Ciên Educ 7:75–88

Teodoro A (2005) Bolonha e a reforma universitária. Dos riscos potenciais às possibilidades de mudança. In: Serralheiro JP (org) O Processo de Bolonha e a Formação dos Educadores e Professores Portugueses. Profedições, Porto, pp 51–57

Union Europea (2010) Estratégia Europa 2020. URL: http://ec.europa.eu/europe2020/indexen.htm

Zeichner K (1993) A formação reflexiva dos professores. Educa, Lisboa

Chapter 7
Concept Mapping to Improve Higher Education

Ignacio Gil Pechuán, M. Pilar Conesa García, and Antonio Navarro-García

Abstract In developing countries, higher education, and particularly university education is recognised as a key force for modernisation and development. This has caused an increase in the demand for its access, accompanied by a number of challenges. This chapter explains the concept mapping methodology to improve university education with the inherent advantage of the combination of qualitative and quantitative techniques, used to get the assessments of quality in higher education, the challenges faced by learners, as well as suggestions for improvement.

7.1 Introduction

Concept mapping can be defined as a pictorial representation combining qualitative and quantitative information which reflects the result of a group's thinking, indicating clusters of ideas by similarity or proximity and their relative importance.

In 1983 Deshpandé argued that research could be qualitative or quantitative, with each option having its advantages and limitations. However, both academic and professional researchers have traditionally tended to use quantitative analysis in their studies. The reason adduced has been an attempt to generalise and objectify the results obtained (Bigné et al. 2002). Nonetheless, the two approaches are not independent or mutually exclusive but rather a continuum that varies from one position to another (Miquel et al. 1997).

I.G. Pechuán (✉) • M.P.C. García
Departamento de Organización de Empresas, Universitat Politècnica de València,
Camino de Vera, 46022 Valencia, Spain
e-mail: igil@doe.upv.es; mconesa1@doe.upv.es

A. Navarro-García
Facultad de CC. Economicas y Empresariales, Departamento de Organización de Empresas y Márketing, Universidad de Sevilla, Avda. Ramón y Cajal, 41018 Sevilla, Valencia, Spain
e-mail: anavarro@us.es

The qualitative paradigm is said to subscribe to a phenomenological, inductive, holistic, subjective, process-oriented and social anthropological world view, while the quantitative paradigm is said to have a positivistic, hypothetic-deductive, particularistic, objective, outcome-oriented, and natural science world view (Reichardt and Cook 1979; Kirk and Miller 1986).

The quantitative method is mainly based on parametric and multivariate statistical analysis, while the qualitative method is based on interviews, group dynamics and behaviour-based observations of the study group. Qualitative analysis looks at processes and meanings while quantitative analysis is based on measurement, values and causal analysis of relationships between variables, and this entails different tools and treatments (Dey 1993; Denzin and Lincoln 1998).

According to Bigné et al. (2002), qualitative research is necessary and useful yet it has an important limitation in terms of methodological approach. This is because this approach is intrinsic to the study itself and furthermore the researcher's subjectivity and intuition are latent, calling into question the validity of the results.

The widespread use of computers in qualitative studies can resolve the differences between qualitative and quantitative methods to bring them closer together (Dey 1993; Denzin and Lincoln 1998). Hence the concept mapping technique to some extent avoids the limitations and uncertainties that may be present in qualitative analysis.

7.2 The Concept Mapping Method

The first reference found is in Trochim and Linton and dates from 1986: "Concept mapping structures the conceptualisation process so that the ideas expressed in the group dynamic can be represented on a perceptual map, which means how these ideas are related to each other can be seen and, optionally, which ideas are more relevant, important, or appropriate". They also define the term "structured conceptualisation" as referring to any process which can be described as a sequence of concrete operationally defined steps and which yields a conceptual representation. Subsequently the same author in 1989 on page 1 fine tunes his definition: "A concept map is a pictorial representation of the group's thinking which displays all of the ideas of the group relative to the topic at hand, shows how these ideas are related to each other and, optionally, shows which ideas are more relevant, important, or appropriate".

Later on, other authors refined the scope of this description, as happened in the 1990s with another definition by Khattri and Miles (1994) in which social interaction is explained: "Concept mapping is a graphic technique for promoting social interaction and exchange by creating the conditions for the understanding of ideas and thoughts and how they might be linked with each other". Bigné et al. (2002), set out the techniques used for analysing concept maps: "Concept mapping's main virtue is to quantify the results of group dynamics by combining it with quantitative techniques such as multidimensional scaling or cluster analysis, thus making the moderator's supervisory work easier". In 2005 a study came out that was more focused on generating ideas and the steps to follow, in which the term is defined as "a multistep process that helps articulate and delineate concepts and their interrelationships through group process (brainstorming, sorting, rating), multivariate statistical analyses (multidimensional scaling, hierarchical cluster analysis), and group interpretation of the conceptual maps produced. The technique's foundation is rooted in cognitive and organisational psychology" (Rosas 2005).

In 2005, Burke et al. summarised what had been indicated up to that point, noting that "it uses inductive and structured group data collection processes which allow for the collection of a wide range of participant-generated ideas and the application of quantitative analytical tools (i.e. multidimensional scaling and hierarchical cluster analysis). Results from the quantitative analysis are used to produce illustrative cluster maps depicting relationships of ideas in the form of clusters. This method provides structure and objectivity to qualitative data". Toral et al. (2006), Nabitz et al. (2007), and Rosas and Camphausen (2007) agree that the technique is a multistage process involving qualitative and quantitative techniques that include knowledge management by a group of experts, multivariate analysis and interpretation of the concept maps resulting from the process. As can be seen, all the authors coincide in the same terms, qualifying the scope of the tools to be used.

7.3 The Concept Mapping Process

Having reviewed the terminological consensus, the overview of the process provided by Trochim (1989) is shown in Fig. 7.1.

7.3.1 Step 1: Preparation

First we had to define the objective to be investigated so as to subsequently choose the subjects to participate in the process. The most common way to do this is to formulate a question agreed by the researchers which clearly shows the information we want to obtain. We then had to decide who the members of the group would be, as their participation has a direct and material effect on the results to be obtained. While including a wide variety of people is recommended in order to enrich the range of views, some studies (Miranda-Gumucio et al. 2013) call for a certain degree of homogeneity of participants, so depending on the study objectives random sampling selection can be used.

As for participants, there is no strict limit on the number of people who should form the group. However, it is suggested that it should be between 10 and 20 people as in the light of the experiences of Trochim (1989) these are the recommended numbers. In our educational case, we chose 17 students to take part in the experiment, so we were within the limit of 15–20 as a manageable group.

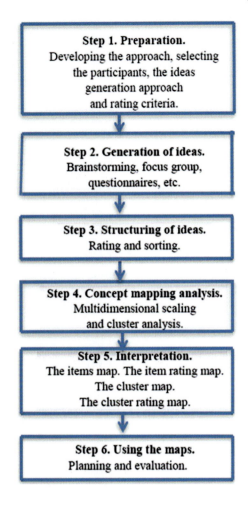

Fig. 7.1 Steps in the concept maps process. *Source*: author's own compilation based on Trochim (1989, p. 3)

Finally, in the preparation stage the scoring scale has to be drawn up to rate the various statements obtained when generating ideas. Every idea is rated separately and individually. The case at hand is an application of the methodology with students doing the "Technological Innovation Management" subject as part of an official University Master's degree programme. The question agreed by the researchers was: "What educational services at the Universidad Politécnica de Valencia do you think could be improved with the use of Innovative technologies"?

The scale chosen for the research was a 1–5 Likert answering the question: "How useful do you think each item is separately"? The ratings were as follows: 1. Completely unessential. 2. Unessential. 3. Neither unessential nor important. 4. Important. 5. Very important. The reason for choosing this scale was that it made it easy for the students to rate each item.

7.3.2 Step 2: Generation of Ideas

The second step begins by explaining the purpose of the group dynamics to the participants. An overview of the stages in the process should also be given. There are a number of in-person and virtual instruments for collecting statements to choose from. They include methods for sharing ideas, brainstorming, focus groups and questionnaires published on the Internet. To this end, a facilitator has to be appointed to coordinate the generation of ideas and the entire experiment, and hence they have to be prepared to guide the statements to a level of conceptual generality and programmatic structure. It is essential that the approach for sharing ideas and rating them is clearly and specifically set out in writing to ensure that each statement represents a single idea.

In the present case the facilitator was one of the researchers. Once the objectives had been clarified, the participants were asked to brainstorm ideas for the concept to be researched. The main objective of this step is to obtain the maximum number of ideas which are refined at the end of it. The experiments carried out by Nabitz et al. (2007) did not involve brainstorming but rather were based on a previous model which was the object of analysis. Simpson (1994) did not use a brainstorming session either and instead worked with a remote focus group and questionnaires. The remaining studies analysed did use brainstorming.

The chosen brainstorming technique consists of giving each participant a number of cards on which they have to write down one idea per card individually. Although the study is anonymous, they also have to state their name on each card in case there are any queries about the idea in the next step. The subjects of the experiment should indicate clear and concise ideas. The facilitator tries not to give out too much information so as to avoid group thinking that would skew valid ideas.

In our case study, a 15-min presentation of the ideas (Pons-Morera et al. 2012) was given to students who were to take part in a brainstorming session with the aim of improving the University's services. Each participant was given several cards in order to write down one idea per card, with their name on each one. They were also told that they should state clear and concise ideas without taking into consideration whether or not they would actually be put into practice. The quantity of information provided was restricted so as to avoid directing their thinking or skewing valid ideas.

7.3.3 Step 3: Structuring of Ideas

Following the ideas generated in the previous step, we then investigated how these ideas were related to each other and their weighting relative to the topic at hand. To do this, participants were first asked to rate each idea separately and individually on the Likert scale specified in the first step.

Once we had as many item scorecards as subjects in the experiment, we drew up a consolidated table of weighted items on the basis of the sum of the individual assessment of each item divided by the number of participating subjects. This is set out in Table 7.1.

		1	2	3	4	5	6	7	8	9	10	11	12	13	14	15	16
									ITEMS								
S U B J E C T S	1	5	4	5	3	2	5	4	4	4	4	4	3	2	3	3	4
	2	3	3	4	3	4	4	5	4	5	4	2	4	2	2	3	3
	3	4	4	4	3	2	4	5	4	5	3	3	4	2	3	2	3
	4	3	4	5	3	1	5	3	3	5	2	5	5	5	4	2	1
	5	4	4	4	4	4	5	5	4	4	3	4	3	3	3	4	4
	6	5	4	2	5	1	3	4	3	4	3	4	3	4	4	5	3
	7	2	1	5	1	1	3	5	4	4	3	4	5	3	3	3	3
	8	4	5	2	4	4	5	5	2	5	3	3	4	3	2	3	3
	9	4	5	5	4	2	4	5	3	5	4	5	5	3	4	2	4
	10	3	4	3	5	1	5	4	2	5	2	2	4	3	3	3	4
	11	3	4	4	4	1	3	5	5	5	4	3	3	3	3	4	4
	12	1	4	4	3	3	3	5	3	4	4	2	4	4	1	3	4
	13	4	5	5	4	4	4	3	3	4	5	3	4	5	5	2	4
	14	5	3	3	4	2	4	4	3	3	4	4	5	3	3	2	2
	15	4	4	5	4	2	5	4	4	4	3	4	4	3	3	3	3
	16	3	3	4	5	2	3	4	4	4	4	5	5	1	3	2	2
	17	4	5	5	4	3	5	5	4	5	4	4	5	3	4	5	4
WEIGHTED SUM		3.58	3.88	4.05	3.70	2.29	4.11	4.41	3.47	4.41	3.47	3.58	4.11	3.05	3.11	3	3.23

Table 7.1 Consolidation or clustering of the weighted assessment of items

Secondly they were asked to group the ideas by families resulting from the brainstorming at their own discretion, while respecting the rules not to put all the ideas in one group, not to make as many groups as there are ideas and to bear in mind that each idea can only go in one group.

The analysis begins with the construction of a similarity matrix $SN \times N$ for each of the participants with N rows by N columns, where N is the total number of ideas generated in the brainstorming session. At the intersection of ideas "i, j" (Si, j) a "1" is placed if the participant put the ideas in the same group, while a "0" indicates that they were not included in the same group. The value of the main diagonal is always "1" because every idea is with itself in the same group (see Table 7.2).

7 Concept Mapping to Improve Higher Education

	1	2	3	4	5	6	7	8	9	10	11	12	13	14	15	16
1	1	1	1	0	0	0	0	0	0	0	0	0	0	1	0	1
2		1	0	0	1	1	0	0	0	0	0	0	1	0	1	1
3			1	0	0	1	1	1	1	0	0	0	0	0	0	0
4				1	0	0	0	0	0	0	0	1	0	0	0	0
5					1	1	0	0	0	0	0	0	1	0	0	0
6						1	0	0	0	0	0	0	0	1	0	0
7							1	1	1	0	0	0	0	0	0	0
8								1	1	0	0	0	0	0	0	0
9									1	0	0	0	0	0	0	0
10										1	0	0	0	0	0	0
11											1	1	0	0	0	0
12												1	0	0	0	0
13													1	0	1	0
14														1	0	0
15															1	0
16																1

Table 7.2 Relationship between items ($S\ 16 \times 16$)

The lower shaded part means that if, for example, item 1 is related to item 3, then item 3 is related to item 1. Next all the $SN \times N$ individual similarity matrices are added to obtain the consolidated matrix, also called the cluster matrix. This cluster matrix also has as many rows and columns as ideas generated in the brainstorming session. However, the number at each intersection ranges from 0 to M, indicating the number of participants out of the total of M participants who have put the pair of ideas in the same group regardless of the approach taken by each individual when forming the cluster.

The value of the main diagonal of the matrix is equal to the total number of participants who have taken part in this stage of the research (Trochim 1993). The cluster matrix provides information about how the participants think the ideas should be grouped. A high value at the intersection of two ideas is indicative that a large number of participants put them together so they are conceptually very close. A low value indicates that few participants have put the ideas in the same cluster and that therefore they are not conceptually clustered.

Once the time stipulated in step 2 for the generation of ideas had elapsed, all the cards were collected and the ideas were numbered and agreed using a computer and projector so everyone could see. Duplicate and invalid ideas were removed in this

Table 7.3 Item assessment

No.	Item	Item assessment
1	Using web 2.0 for interaction between lecturers and students. Guided tutorials. Implementation on the University Intranet	1–5
2	Audiovisual support in classes to better explain the subject	1–5
3	Companies-UPV Intranet. Part of the syllabus recommended by companies	1–5
4	Repository of student notes and work, supervised by lecturers	1–5
5	Video library of films related to subjects, in order to discuss them afterwards	1–5
6	Classes taught by experts by videoconferencing	1–5
7	Free use of practice classrooms so students can carry out new and innovative projects in their spare time	1–5
8	Laboratory for a specific technique in a particular subject to improve the way it is studied (subject without a laboratory). Laboratory 1	1–5
9	Laboratory for studying new materials and applying ideas. Laboratory 2	1–5
10	Add languages to the University's website (German, French, etc.)	1–5
11	Informative sessions to show students the technological services offered by the University (in addition to those for the Master's programme)	1–5
12	Scanning books so students can consult them online	1–5
13	Student pushbuttons to answer questions asked in class in real time and get statistics (Buzz PlayStation)	1–5
14	Tutoring via Skype or a similar system	1–5
15	Using a digital whiteboard to improve the assimilation of content and help lecturers with their teaching	1–5
16	Video and/or audio recordings of classes uploaded to the Intranet (to see them again)	1–5

step. In some cases, we had to ask the person who had come up with an idea as we were unable to work out what they meant, which justified why participants had to put their name on each card. In this way we drew up an agreed list of 16 ideas or items that resulted in Table 7.3.

Once the clusters or families had been made, the participants were asked to give a name to each one based on their view of its contents. The facilitator then collected each participant's clusters once they had finished, thanked them for their time and thus concluded the session. The researchers then drew up a consolidated or clustered table by summing all the individual tables (see Table 7.3) and dividing them by the number of participants so that in the end we had a single table (see Table 7.1) with the total weighted cluster scores for each item.

Subsequently square, binary and symmetrical Table 7.2 were produced for each cluster of individual ideas in which a 0 indicates that two ideas are not related (in the same family) and 1 indicates that they are. After making as many Table 7.2 as there were subjects, the consolidated or clustered table required to continue with the method was produced (see Table 7.4). This table is the result of the (cumulative) sum of the (individual) square, binary and symmetric matrices, so that the diagonal unequivocally corresponds with the number of participants (17 in the case at hand).

We ended this step by obtaining the two consolidated Tables 7.1 and 7.4 showing the outcome of the research, thus completing our initial goal of structuring ideas.

7 Concept Mapping to Improve Higher Education

	1	2	3	4	5	6	7	8	9	10	11	12	13	14	15	16
1	17	8	5	8	2	11	1	1	1	5	7	7	4	17	5	15
2	8	17	3	5	10	12	0	1	1	2	3	3	9	7	14	13
3	5	3	17	2	2	8	3	3	3	1	3	2	1	3	0	3
4	8	5	2	17	0	4	2	2	2	2	4	12	3	2	3	9
5	2	10	2	0	17	5	0	1	0	1	1	1	1	2	3	3
6	11	12	8	4	5	17	1	3	2	2	3	3	5	9	6	10
7	1	0	3	2	0	1	17	13	14	1	2	1	1	1	1	1
8	1	1	3	2	1	3	13	17	16	3	2	3	0	0	2	0
9	1	1	3	2	0	2	14	16	17	2	2	2	2	1	3	2
10	5	2	1	2	1	2	1	3	2	17	7	2	1	1	2	2
11	7	3	3	4	1	3	2	2	2	7	17	7	4	3	3	3
12	7	3	2	12	1	3	1	3	2	2	7	17	1	2	2	6
13	4	9	1	3	1	5	1	0	2	1	4	1	17	1	5	1
14	17	7	3	2	2	9	1	0	1	1	3	2	1	17	4	5
15	5	14	0	3	3	6	1	2	3	2	3	2	5	4	17	7
16	15	13	3	9	3	10	1	0	2	2	3	6	1	5	7	17

Table 7.4 Consolidated table on the relation between items ($S\ 16 \times 16$)

7.3.4 Step 4: Concept Map Analysis

In this stage (Trochim 1989) the ideas obtained are represented and this involves three steps. First, we conduct an analysis that locates each statement as a separate point on the point rating map. This analysis is performed using a combined dissimilarity matrix that is subjected to two-dimensional multidimensional scaling. The points representing each impact are distributed in the space so that the distances between pairs of points have the maximum possible relation with the similarity attributed by the managers. Thus two similar impacts are represented by nearby points and vice versa (Fernández 1991). If the items are closer to each other, it means that they have been grouped more frequently. If two ideas are separated, it means that few subjects have thought they are in the same group of ideas.

In concept mapping, multidimensional scaling analysis creates a map of points that represent the set of statements generated in the brainstorming based on the similarity matrix resulting from the classification. The second analysis which is conducted to represent the conceptual domain is called hierarchical cluster analysis

Table 7.5 Resulting clusters

Cluster 1	Cluster 2	Cluster 3
1: Using web 2.0	4: Notes repository	7: Free use of classrooms
2: Audiovisual support	10: Add languages to website	8: Laboratory 1
3: Companies-UPV Intranet	11: Informative sessions	9: Laboratory 2
5: Film-cinema forum	12: Scanning books	
6: Videoconference classes		
13: Student pushbuttons		
14: Tutoring via Skype		
15: Digital whiteboard		
16: Video recordings of classes		

(Anderberg 1973; Everitt 1980). This analysis is used to group individual statements on the map into clusters of statements which presumably reflect similar concepts.

There are a large number of applications called mind maps or conceptual maps available on the market (Tramullas et al. 2009). In the present case, the data were entered into the SPSS computer program to conduct multidimensional scaling, so that we defined the 16 items as numeric economic variables labelled by the 17 participating subjects. This gave us a first draft of what became our representation of concept mapping.

To perform the second analysis indicated by the method, we conducted cluster analysis. We tested three clusters, since most of the participants grouped the items into three groups to give the clusters set out in Table 7.5.

Having analysed all the results, we found a total of six scenarios: combinations of three and four clusters with the average linkage, nearest neighbour and Ward methods. Based on criteria for matching results and their logical interpretation, the group obtained from three clusters using the average linkage method was chosen.

The final analysis of the method in this step involved drawing up our concept map by grouping items into three weighted clusters, i.e. by adding up the value of the weighted items in each cluster obtained in the consolidated table and then dividing them by the number of items contained in that cluster. This gives Fig. 7.2, where the number of each cluster (1,2,3) appears with its weighted value.

7.3.5 Step 5: Interpreting Maps

As we saw in the previous section, we grouped the ideas into three clusters. The first cluster is formed by the following nine items: 1: Using web 2.0 for interaction between lecturers and students. Guided tutorials. Implementation in multiple formats, 2: Audiovisual support in classes to better explain the subject, 3: Companies-UPV Intranet. Part of the syllabus recommended by companies, 5: Video library of film-related subjects, in order to discuss them afterwards, 6: Classes taught by experts by videoconferencing, 12: GIS concerning administrative procedures with internal privileges, but with restricted access for the public, 13: Student pushbuttons

7 Concept Mapping to Improve Higher Education 71

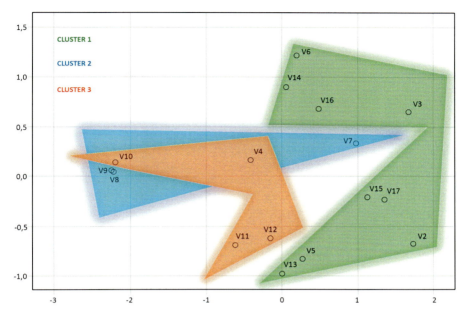

Fig. 7.2 Concept mapping. Cluster 1 (3.36): Using technology laboratories for teaching and innovative purposes. Cluster 2 (3.71): Teaching support technological services. Cluster 3 (4.09): Teaching technological services for everyday use in the classroom

to answer questions asked in class in real time and get statistics (Buzz PlayStation), 14: Tutoring via Skype or a similar system, 15: Using a digital whiteboard to improve the assimilation of content and help lecturers with their teaching, 16: Video and/or audio recordings of classes uploaded to the multi-format platform.

The second cluster is made up of the following four items: 4: Repository of student notes and work, supervised by lecturers, 10: Add languages to the UPV website (German, French, etc.), 11: Informative sessions to show students the technological services offered by the UPV, 12: Scanning books so students can consult them online.

Finally, the third cluster is made up of the final three items: 7: Free use of practice classrooms so students can carry out new and innovative projects in their spare time, 8: Laboratory 1 for a specific technique in a particular subject to improve the way it is studied, for teaching purposes, 9: Laboratory 2 for studying new materials and applying ideas. An analysis of the weighted perceptual map shows that items 8 and 9 are very close, noting that the seventh item is not as close which may be explained by a flat transposition of the points in the space. The three resulting clusters have been named based on the items forming each cluster.

We started by labelling the third cluster, the first to be formed, as using technology laboratories for teaching and innovative purposes. Looking at Fig. 7.1, we see that this cluster has a weighted score of 4.09 out of 5, the highest of the three resulting clusters. This cluster retains its items in all the methods used, which means that they are closely related.

The second cluster, with a score of 3.71 out of 5, could be called teaching support technological services. Therefore cluster no. 1 can clearly be called teaching technological services for everyday use in the classroom, with a weighted score of 3.36 out of 5.

7.3.6 Step 6: Using the Maps

In the sixth step, the maps are used as a pictorial representation of an explanation by a group of experts about a particular concept, meaning a theoretical representation of the experts' opinions in this regard. In the present case, concept mapping will be used to improve educational services in the University's Master's degree programme with priority assigned by the financial possibilities of the most representative ideas.

7.4 Conclusion

Concept mapping is a very valuable tool for use in many fields of study in order to identify the key points of a system or organisation. In this chapter we have discussed it in terms of its application to a particular subject on an official Master's degree programme, since as we have shown its application makes it possible to obtain both qualitative and quantitative information.

Analysis of the weighted scores of the items shows that the ideas which students thought most important were number 7: Free use of practice classrooms so students can carry out new and innovative projects in their spare time, and number 9: Laboratories 1 and 2 for studying new materials and applications, with the same weighted scores of 4.41 out of 5.

We also found that the students identified the third cluster as the most important one, which means using laboratories to carry out teaching and innovation projects are perceived as one of the best uses of technology for teaching.

It should be noted that the application of the above methodology with the students has been highly satisfactory. As we had subjects with academic training and a classroom with enough computers and a projector, we could digitally fill in the above tables which greatly simplified the brainstorming session.

References

Anderberg MR (1973) Cluster analysis for applications. Academic, New York
Bigné JE, Aldás J, Küster I, Vila N (2002) Estableciendo los determinantes de la fidelidad del cliente: Un estudio basado en técnicas cualitativas. Invest Market 77:58–62
Burke JG, O'Campo P, Peak GL, Gielen AC, McDonnell KA, Trochim WMK (2005) An introduction to concept mapping as a participatory public health research method. Qual Health Res 15(10):1392–1410

Denzin NK, Lincoln YS (1998) Collecting and interpreting qualitative material. Sage, Thousand Oaks, CA

Dey I (1993) Qualitative data analysis. Routledge, London

Everitt B (1980) Cluster analysis. Halsted Press, Wiley, New York, NY

Fernández O (1991) El análisis de Cluster: Aplicación, interpretación y validación. Papers 37:65–76

Khattri N, Miles GL (1994) Cognitive mapping: a review and working guide. Center for Policy Research, Sparkhill, NY

Kirk J, Miller ML (1986) Reliability and validity in qualitative research. Sage, Beverly Hills, CA

Miranda-Gumucio L, Gil-Pechuán I, Palacios-Marqués D (2013) An exploratory study of the determinants of switching and loyalty in prepaid cell phone users. An application of concept mapping. Serv Bus 7(4):603–622

Miquel S, Bigné E, Lévy JP, Cuenca AC, Miquel MJ (1997) Investigación de Mercados. McGraw-Hill, Madrid

Nabitz U, Severens P, Brink WVD, Jansen P (2007) Improving the EFQM model: an empirical study on model development and theory building using concept mapping. Total Qual Manage 12(1):69–81

Pons-Morera C, Canós-Darós L, Gil Pechuán I (2012) Diagrama de afinidad aplicado a mejorar los servicios tecnológicos de la Universidad Politécnica de Valencia. Working papers on operations management (WPOM) 3(1):46–60. ISSN: 1989–9068

Reichardt CS, Cook TD (1979) Beyond qualitative versus quantitative methods. In: Cook TD, Reichardt CS (eds) Qualitative and quantitative methods in evaluation research. Sage, Beverly Hills, CA, pp 7–32

Rosas SR (2005) Concept mapping as a technique for program theory development: an illustration using family support programs. Am J Eval 26(3):389–401

Rosas SR, Camphausen LC (2007) The use of concept mapping for scale development and validation in evaluation. Eval Program Plann 30:125–135

Simpson B (1994) How do women scientists perceive their own career development? Int J Career Manage 6(1):19–27

Tramullas J, Sánchez-Casabón AI, Garrido-Picazo P (2009) Gestión de información personal con software para mapas conceptuales. El Prof Inform 18(6):601–612

Trochim WMK (1989) An introduction to concept mapping for planning and evaluation. Eval Program Plann 12(1):1–16

Trochim WMK (1993) The reliability of concept mapping. In the minutes of the annual conference of the American Evaluation Association, Dallas, TX

Trochim WMK, Linton R (1986) Conceptualization for planning and evaluation. Eval Program Plann 9(4):289–308

Toral SL, Barrero F, Martinez MR, Gallardo S, Cortés FJ (2006) Determinación de las variables de diseño en el desarrollo de una herramienta de e-learning. Pixel-Bit, revista de medios y educación 27:99–113

Chapter 8
Students' Performance with the Introduction of the Bologna Process: An Approach Via Quantile Regression

Ana Fernández-Sainz, Jose Domingo García-Merino, and Sara Urionabarrenetxea-Zabalandikoetxea

Abstract This paper seeks to determine whether the introduction of new degrees under the European Higher Education Area has brought about any improvement in students' performance, based on an extended concept of performance and an analysis of the core values and distribution tails, i.e. distinguishing between the improvements achieved by excellent students and by average students. Quantile regression analysis is combined with a least squeres ordinaries (OLS) approach to estimate students' performance. This method is able to capture the extreme behaviour at both tails of students' performance distribution. An empirical study is conducted on students' grades in the subject Business Management: Introduction at the University of the Basque Country (Spain). Our principal finding is that although OLS estimation indicates that there is no significant improvement in students' performance, the results for quantile regression show that in the 25 % quantile final grades increase significantly, while in the extreme deciles (95 %) their performance decrease.

A. Fernández-Sainz
Facultad de Cc. Económicas y Empresariales, Departamento Economía Aplicada III (Econometría y Estadística), Universidad del País Vasco/Euskal Herriko Unibertsitatea, Avda. Lehendakari Aguirre, 48015 Bilbao, Spain
e-mail: ana.fernandez@ehu.es

J.D. García-Merino (✉) • S. Urionabarrenetxea-Zabalandikoetxea
Facultad de Cc. Económicas y Empresariales, Departamento Economía Financiera II (Economía de la Empresa y Comercialización), Universidad del País Vasco/Euskal Herriko Unibertsitatea, Avda. Lehendakari Aguirre, 48015 Bilbao, Spain
e-mail: josedomingo.garcia@ehu.es; sara.urionabarrenetxea@ehu.es

8.1 Introduction

The creation of the European Higher Education Area (EHEA) has entailed major challenges for all European universities. The Declaration Sorbonne Joint (1998) stated that the all European Universities's objective must be to consolidate, which should be reflected in student outcomes.

The studies conducted to gauge whether the Bologna process has actually brought about an improvement in performance (Herrero and Algarrada 2010; Florido et al. 2011; Valveny et al. 2012) have tended to suffer from two limitations: they have focused on a single dimension of performance (the final grades) and they analyse improvements solely in terms of the average grades obtained. This average-based estimation may fail to capture one crucial aspect: the fact that the changes introduced may impact differently on the performance of excellent students and that of average students (Eide and Showalter 1998).

Our purpose here is to compare whether the introduction of new degrees under the EHEA has actually improved the performance of students. Added value is provided in two areas: firstly, the concept of student performance is adapted to current context; and secondly, an inter-quartile analysis (Chen et al. 2012) is conducted with a view to obtaining a fuller picture of the outcomes achieved.

The paper is structured as follows: firstly, we examine the EHEA as an opportunity for improving the students' performance. After that we set out the hypotheses. Then we explain the method used in our study, defining the sample population, the scales used for measurement and the procedure. Subsequently, we present and discuss our main results. Finally, we sum up our conclusions.

8.2 Students' Performance Beyond the Average Grade Obtained

The EHEA is a response to a new social order in which knowledge has become provisional to the extent that its transfer is no longer enough. A graduate cannot be just a repository of knowledge, so courses cannot be only based on the transmission of contents (Valveny et al. 2012); rather, and students must be provided with useful skills for their professional career. It was under this approach that the concept of competency-based learning emerged. Competencies do not displace knowledge: they complement it to form an all-round system that is better suited to improving future education. Competencies refer to applied knowledge, so competency-based learning means knowing, understanding and using knowledge (Jones et al. 2009).

Tovar et al. (2007) analyse 94 experiences at Spanish universities and observe that the process of adapting to Bologna has entailed two major pedagogical changes in the teaching/learning process: new teaching methods and new assessment systems. Both are defined in line with the competencies to be attained.

In terms of teaching methods, competency-based learning calls for an approach that is centred more on students: each student must take responsibility for their own learning, so students need to play a more dynamic role and participate more in the process (Gil et al. 2013). Participative and collaborative methodologies have been introduced that seek to focus on developing not just technical but also other types of competency (Gil et al. 2013). These methodologies have many advantages: they increase students' motivation, facilitate more meaningful learning, encourage critical and creative thinking and promote interaction, thus honing interpersonal skills.

In regard to the changes in the assessment system the first point that must be stressed is that assessment is an important issue that affects the whole of the learning process (Martínez-Lirola and Rubio 2009). Conventional assessment methods seek to assess the acquired knowledge at the final stage of learning. The need to assess the learning process itself has led to the development of the continuous assessment system, in which there is more feedback between faculty and students, turning assessment into one more stage in the learning process.

After the implementation of the process, studies intended to gauge its impact on the performance of students began to be published. However, two issues have yet to be examined: the potential differences in the impact of the new pedagogical requirements associated with the Bologna process on the performance of excellent students and average students; and the idea of improved performance being reflected not just in the grade obtained in a final exam but through an approach focused on autonomous-learning and the acquisition of competencies.

In regard to the first of these issues, the collaborative work and active methodologies which are such mainstays of the Bologna process may result in greater improvements in performance among excellent students, since part of the success of such methods lies in motivating students to take part in groups and to share ideas (de Graaff and Kolmos 2007), and it is excellent students who have the highest intrinsic level of motivation to learn (Yip 2009). However, a difficulty that arises in the implementation of collaborative work is that tasks are not always shared out equally among all members of the group (Macho and Elejalde 2013): opportunist behaviour may arise. Students with the potential to attain higher grades and levels of learning may be held back by the behaviour and performance of other group members.

Continuous assessment systems entail a greater, more regularly distributed workload for students than conventional assessment systems (Capó et al. 2013), which may have a negative effect on more irregular students. But they could also have the opposite effect: continuous assessment systems develop extrinsic motivation mechanisms linked to the obtaining of a better grade that have been shown to be significant for students who take a superficial learning approach (precisely the type of approach most widely observed among average students) (Gargallo et al. 2012).

In regard to the second issue, the most used indicator of students' performance has traditionally been their grades (Florido et al. 2011). This single indicator does not seem to capture the essence of the Bologna process, which is based precisely on autonomous-learning and the acquisition of competencies. Moreover, it is not enough to consider the perspective of the faculty alone, because students with different backgrounds, intellectual capabilities, motivations and levels of dedication will not behave in the same way. It therefore seems necessary also to include the students' perspective. Knowledge is meaningful if the student is capable of applying it, i.e. it is the student who gives meaning to the learning undertaken. Therefore, as pointed out by Smith et al. (2011), a combination of direct measurements (assessing students' mastery of content or skills) and indirect measurements (i.e. assessing opinions or attitudes toward learning) of performance is needed to determine whether students are "successful" on a course. The information added by the two indicators is not redundant because, as shown by some studies, the correlation between them is low (Kamphorst et al. 2013).

From the perspective of faculty, Bologna supplements the traditional dimension associated with cognitive elements measured via the grading of a final exam by requiring that the work of each student be taken as a unit of reference. This calls for new methods of assessment based on the effort put in by students. Thus, the second dimension to be considered is continuous assessment (Sanchez-Elez et al. 2013).

It is important that students themselves should assess the extent to which they feel that they have attained their learning objectives and developed the competencies associated with the qualification that they are studying. How they perceive their level of competency acquisition should be a crucial indicator of the suitability of all the changes proposed. Starting from the classification set out in *Tuning Educational Structures in Europe* (González and Wagenaar 2003), we have grouped competencies under the headings of Instrumental, Systemic and Interpersonal and asked students themselves to assess them.

8.3 Hypotheses

We have conducted an empirical analysis using the subject of In Business Management: Introduction at the University of the Basque Country (UPV/EHU) as our case study. This subject has been brought into line with the requirements of the Bologna process, and can therefore be taken as representative of what may happen in other cases.

The reforms introduced under the Bologna process are intended to raise the standard of the teaching/learning process, and they need to be backed up by results. Our main hypothesis is therefore as follows:

Main hypothesis: "Students perform better now that the process of adaptation to the EHEA has been implemented".

Based on the broad definition of "performance" mentioned in the previous section, this main hypothesis breaks down into various sub-hypotheses:

H_1: The grades obtained by students have improved under the system introduced by the Bologna process.
H_2: Self-assessment by students of the competencies acquired has improved under the system introduced by Bologna process.
H_3: Performance has not improved to the same extent at all the different distribution levels.

8.4 Econometric Method

8.4.1 The Population and the Sample Studied

To check out the hypotheses put forward for this purpose, we monitored the performance of the 596 students who took Business Management: Introduction at the UPV/EHU in the last academic year prior to the implementation of the Bologna process (2009–2010) and that of the 680 in the first year of its implementation (2010–2011). To obtain students' self-assessments a questionnaire was drawn up. Five hundred and seventy-eight valid replies to this questionnaire were received: 232 for the pre-Bologna year and 346 for the Bologna year. This represents a confidence level of 95 %, with a maximum error level of 3 %.

8.4.2 Scales of Measurement

In line with the hypotheses put forward, the performance of students is assessed via two complementary indicators.

- The grade awarded by faculty: this is obtained by direct measurement, considering (a) the grade awarded in the final exam; and (b) the grade awarded in continuous assessment throughout the year.
- Self-assessment by students of the acquired competences (instrumental, systemic and interpersonal): this is obtained via a preliminary Principal Component Analysis based on the answers given to a questionnaire using a Likert type 1–5 scale.

8.4.3 Procedure

Our approach is based on quantile regressions, which estimate the effect of explanatory variables on the dependent variable at different points of the latter's conditional distribution (Koenker and Bassett 1978). Since we are not merely interested in the conditional mean performance but also the extreme performances, to obtain a more complete picture we also consider several different regression curves that correspond to the various percentage points of the distributions and not only the conditional mean distribution, which neglects the extreme points of the relationship between variables. Thus, the quantile regression methodology of Koenker and Bassett (1978) is applied here.

A general method for estimating models of conditional quantile functions can be expressed as the solution to a simple optimisation problem underlying the least squeres model. The quantile regression model for the τth conditional quantile of Y is:

$$Y_i = X_i'\beta(\tau) + \mu_i(\tau) \quad \text{and} \quad Q_\tau(Y|X_i) = X_i'\beta(\tau)$$

where $Q_\tau(Y|X_i)$ is the τth conditional quantile of Y, $\beta(\tau)$ are the regression quantile coefficients and $0 < \tau < 1$ is the τ quantile.

It is clear that $\beta_j(\tau) = \partial Q_\tau(Y|X)/\partial X_j$, the estimation of the regression quantiles' coefficients, $\beta(\tau)$, can differ across τ, so the marginal effect of a particular explanatory variable may not be homogeneous across different quantiles. It is important to note that a quantile regression model proposes different regression lines for different levels of the conditional distribution of Y. Parameter estimates in linear quantile regression models have the same interpretation as those in any linear regression model.

8.5 Results

Our results are presented in the order in which the hypotheses are set out: those from the perspective of faculty are shown first and the opinions of students themselves about their learning process. Then differences being established on the different distribution levels are analysed.

The initial idea is to check whether the performance of students improves. Our results show that on average there is no statistically significant improvement in final or continuous assessment grades (Table 8.1). The only statistically significant increase is in exam grades. Nor is there an improvement in the total competencies. However, when distinctions are drawn between types of competency a significant improvement is found in systemic competencies, i.e. those concerned with capability for autonomous-learning which may be those which are encouraged most by active methods. There is a drop in instrumental competencies, i.e. those related most closely with the acquisition of new knowledge.

The results vary if the quartile analysis is realised. The students in the 5th percentile do significantly worse in their final grades, mainly because their continuous assessment grades are lower (Table 8.4). The increased weight of continuous assessment in the final grade, together with the increase in workload that this entails, results in numerous tasks going unfinished, which in turn leads to heavier penalties under the Bologna system. However, the process does result in significantly better final grades (Table 8.2) in the 25th percentile. This improvement is due mainly to significant increases in the grades obtained in continuous assessment (Table 8.4). In the 95th percentile the process of adaptation results in lower grades as a result of lower scores in continuous assessment.

Exam grades improve significantly among students in the 75th percentile (Table 8.3), which indicates that the more regular effort and greater discipline applied by these good students bear fruit in their exam grades.

Continuous assessment grades are significantly better in both the 25th and 50th percentiles, indicating that the greater extrinsic incentives (the greater weight of continuous assessment in the overall grade) introduced by the Bologna process have a positive effect on results (Table 8.4).

Table 8.1 OLS regression

	Final grade	Exam grade	Continuous assessment grade	Total competency	Instrumental competency	Systemic competency	Interpersonal competency
Constant	6.19 (46.02)***	4.92 (48.44)***	5.95 (37.88)***	5.63 (56.09)***	6.37 (62.67)***	5.36 (43.49)***	6.80 (45.76)***
Bologna	0.03 (0.19)	0.32 (2.43)**	0.28 (1.30)	0.12 (0.95)	−0.33 (2.61)**	0.49 (3.18)***	0.18 (0.96)

Note: t statistics in parentheses; **$p<0.05$, ***$p<0.01$

Table 8.2 Quantile regression final grade

	5 %	25 %	50 %	75 %	95 %
Constant	4.08 (5.86)***	4.91 (22.02)***	5.95 (26.26)***	6.80 (18.48)***	9.89 (29.66)***
Bologna	−0.75 (1.80)*	0.32 (2.40)***	0.20 (1.48)	0.300 (1.36)	−0.69 (3.47)***

Note: t statistics in parentheses; *$p<0.10$, ***$p<0.01$

Table 8.3 Quantile regression exam grade

	5 %	25 %	50 %	75 %	95 %
Constant	2.42 (7.72)***	3.74 (11.51)***	4.59 (14.98)***	5.11 (11.15)***	7.73 (17.21)***
Bologna	0.08 (0.44)	0.22 (1.11)	0.24 (1.34)	0.67 (2.46)***	0.01 (0.03)

Note: t statistics in parentheses; ***$p<0.01$

Table 8.4 Quantile regression continuous assessment grade

	5 %	25 %	50 %	75 %	95 %
Constant	3.85 (3.75)***	2.45 (4.58)***	5.28 (11.58)***	7.60 (20.98)***	9.95 (84.81)***
Bologna	−1.93 (3.14)***	1.53 (4.78)***	0.93 (3.41)***	0.20 (0.93)	−0.35 (2.18)***

Note: t statistics in parentheses; ***$p<0.01$

Table 8.5 Quantile regression total competencies

	5 %	25 %	50 %	75 %	95 %
Constant	3.08 (14.136)***	4.62 (33.83)***	5.77 (52.89)***	6.54 (31.95)***	8.08 (24.74)***
Bologna	0.39 (1.37)	0.38 (2.21)*	0.00	0.00	0.00

Note: t statistics in parentheses; *$p<0.1$, ***$p<0.01$

Analogous results are obtained for the total competencies (Table 8.5): there is a statistically significant improvement only in the 25th percentile.

8.6 Discussion

A percentile-based analysis reveals that significant improvements are obtained in the final grades of students in the 25th percentile, especially in continuous assessment grades. This can be explained by two reasons: firstly, the increased weight of continuous assessment in the final grade means that there is more incentive to work steadily day by day. This modifies students' behaviour patterns and helps them to become more involved in learning. Once they have invested a substantial time in the subject the cost of giving up becomes greater than if they have done little work and the final exam is still pending. They are therefore more likely to continue making progress.

Secondly, the fact that continuous assessment is conducive to collaborative work means that less motivated students are "dragged long" by team dynamics and end up involving themselves more, which is positive in terms of their results. By contrast, the final grades of excellent students are lower, perhaps because their continuous assessment grades are lower. This can also be explained by two reasons: firstly, as pointed out above, they have to spend part of their time helping less able students, which leaves them less time to hone their own work. Secondly, competency-based assessment calls for more skills and requires that they be evidenced for longer than the conventional system, in which a show of ability on the day of the final exam sufficed to earn them top marks and in general only technical knowledge and skills were tested. This makes it harder to obtain the highest grades.

A significant improvement in final exam grades is observed in the students in the 75th percentile. In the conventional system these students may obtain good grades but their lack of consistency means that they shine less in final exams. The greater discipline and gradual assimilation of knowledge entailed by continuous assessment are reflected in their performance in such exams.

It is also significant that students themselves perceive their main improvement as coming in systemic competencies, and believe themselves to be worse off in instrumental competencies. This result is not a problem: the rate at which knowledge becomes obsolete means that nowadays it is crucial to develop skills concerned with the ability to learn, i.e. skills associated with systemic competencies. One of the main virtues of the new paradigm is therefore a performance improvement in terms of developing systemic competencies. As students spend more time during the year working on this type of competencies, they may have less time left for acquiring new knowledge, which may explain why performance in instrumental competences is down. However the increased emphasis on gradual, regular learning may also mean that students are not actually aware of how much they have really learned during the year. In the conventional system, the acquisition of new knowledge is often associated with revision leading up to the final exam: at that time there is a "leap forward" in students' perceived acquisition of knowledge. Indeed, the improvement in the grades awarded by faculty (Table 8.2) is greater than that perceived by students (Table 8.5), and the gap between them is at its widest at the top end of the distribution range.

Another noteworthy point is that students themselves believe that they have improved little in the development of interpersonal skills, even though the new system stresses collaborative work and seeks to foster communication skills, etc. It must be borne in mind that the more group work there is, the more potential there is for conflict. This may lead to negative feelings and some degree of rejection of group work, which in turn may affect the way in which students perceive their level of development of interpersonal competencies. However, it must also be acknowledged that self-regulation is not easy to achieve in groups: it may call for a level of personal maturity that first-year students have yet to acquire. Numerous studies have noted that the development of co-operation dynamics is closely linked to the emotional maturity of group members (Johnson and Johnson 2009).

8.7 Conclusions

The changes brought about by adaptation to the EHEA in terms of reconfiguring both the teaching/learning and assessment processes have resulted in certain improvements in students' performance.

The pedagogical changes introduced include active methodologies based on collaborative learning and the implementation of continuous assessment systems. These changes have improved the performance of below-average students (the 25th percentile): having to make an effort more consistently has enabled them to raise their continuous assessment grades, and this improvement is reflected in their final grades. Improvements are also observed in students' perception of their acquisition of systemic competencies, e.g. those concerned with the ability to continue learning throughout their careers.

However, the Bologna process also has its downside: it is harder for students to obtain top grades. The increased weight of collaborative work makes it harder to distinguish between team members, which means that excellent students (those in the 95th percentile) see their continuous assessment grades worsen, and with them their final grades. Besides, students feel that they have not improved in terms of acquiring instrumental competencies. The new system fosters the development of skills in lifelong learning, at the expense of the acquisition of new knowledge.

In short, the new system has resulted in objective improvements but there needs to be a change in culture to facilitate their assimilation, and the assessment system also needs to be adjusted.

Acknowledgment The authors acknowledge financial support from FESIDE Foundation, Econometrics Research Group (Basque Government grant IT-642-13), and Educational Innovation Project (University of the Basque Country PIE-6380)-University of the Basque Country.

References

Capó J, Oliver X, Sard M (2013) Evaluando la evaluación continua. Rev Innov Educ 10:33–43

Chen ST, Kuo HI, Chen CC (2012) Estimating the extreme behaviors of students performance using quantile regression—evidences from Taiwan. Educ Econ 20(1):93–113

de Graaff E, Kolmos A (2007) History of problem-based and project-based learning. In: de Graaff E, Kolmos A (eds) Management of change: implementation of problem-based and project-based learning in engineering. Sense Publisher, Rotterdam, pp 1–8

Declaration Sorbonne Joint (1998) Joint declaration on harmonisation of the architecture of the European higher education system. http://www.ehea.info/Uploads/Declarations/SORBONNE_DECLARATION1.pdf. Accessed 12 Nov 2013

Eide E, Showalter MH (1998) The effect of school quality on student performance: a quantile regression approach. Econ Lett 58:345–350

Florido C, Jiménez JL, Santana I (2011) Obstáculos en el camino hacia Bolonia: Efectos de la implantación del Espacio Europeo de la Educación Superior (EEES) sobre los resultados académicos. Rev Educ 354:629–656

Gargallo B, Suárez JM, García E, Pérez C, Sahuquillo PM (2012) Enfoques de aprendizaje en estudiantes universitarios excelentes y en estudiantes medios. Rev Esp Pedagog 70(252):185–200

Gil C, Montoya MG, Herrada RI, Baños R, Montoya FG (2013) Engaging students in computer-supported cooperative learning. Int J Learn Technol 8(3):297–311

González J, Wagenaar R (2003) Tuning educational structures in Europe. Final report. Phase one. Universidad de Deusto, Bilbao

Herrero I, Algarrada I (2010) Is the new ECTS system better than the traditional one? An application to the ECTS pilot-project at the University Pablo de Olavide. Eur J Oper Res 204(1):164–172

Johnson DW, Johnson RT (2009) An educational psychology success story: social interdependence theory and cooperative learning. Educ Res 38:365–379

Jones M, Coiacetto E, Jackson J, Coote M, Steele W, Budge T, Gall S (2009) Generating academic standards and assessment practices in work integrated learning: a case study from urban and regional planning. Asia Pac J Coop Educ 10(3):203–215

Kamphorst JC, Hofman WHA, Jansen EPWA, Terlouw C (2013) The relationship between perceived competence and earned credits in competence-based higher education. Assess Eval High Educ 38(6):646–661

Koenker R, Bassett G (1978) Regression quantiles. Econometrica 46(1):33–50

Macho E, Elejalde MJ (2013) Case study of a problem-based learning course of physics in a telecommunications engineering degree. Eur J Eng Educ 38(4):408–416

Martínez-Lirola M, Rubio F (2009) Students' beliefs about portfolio evaluation and its influence on their learning outcomes to develop EFL in a Spanish context. Int J Engl Stud 9(1):91–111

Sanchez-Elez M, Pardines I, Garcia P, Miñana G, Roman S, Sanchez M, Risco JL (2013) Enhancing students' learning process through self-generated tests. J Sci Educ Technol 22:1–11

Smith P, Dunn S, Pollock D, Stewart M, Galivan C (2011) Enhance, engage, evolve: challenges, rewards, and the culture of evidence in online learning. In: Fourth SoTL commons: a conference for the scholarship of teaching & learning, Georgia, 9–11 March 2011

Tovar E, Plaza I, Castro M, Llamas M, Arcega F, Jurado F, Mur F, Sánchez JA, Falcone F, Domínguez M (2007) Modeling the best practices towards the adaptation to the European credit transfer system in technical degrees within the IEEE ES chapter. In: Proceedings of 37th annual conference frontiers in education conference-global engineering, Milwaukee, 10–13 Oct 2007

Valveny E, Benavente R, Lapedriza À, Ferrer M, Garcia-Barnés J, Sánchez G (2012) Adaptation of a computer programming course to the ESHE requirements: evaluation five years later. Eur J Eng Educ 37(3):243–254

Yip MC (2009) Differences between high and low academic achieving university students in learning and study strategies: a further investigation. Educ Res Eval 15(6):561–570

Chapter 9
Exploring the Use of an ICT-Based Tool for Assessing Competencies in Postgraduate Students

Fariza Achcaoucaou, Santiago Forgas-Coll, and Ramon Palau-Saumell

Abstract The construction of the European Higher Education Area (EHEA) has brought in several profound changes in the university environment. Skills learning methodologies are one of the central issues of this new educational paradigm. Spanish universities have been very careful in defining the competencies that students must achieve on the new degrees and postgraduate courses. However, they have paid less attention to the question of how these competencies should be measured. The present study addresses this issue by examining the implementation of a competency assessment tool. Specifically, we analyse the status of soft skills among students on the Official Master's programme 'Creating and Managing Innovative Technology-Based Companies' at the University of Barcelona, using the Evolute system developed by the Tampere University of Technology (Finland). The results show the Evolute methodology to be an appropriate tool for data collection and analysis. The system is ideal for helping managers of higher education to analyse and evaluate their students' skills acquisition.

F. Achcaoucaou • S. Forgas-Coll (✉)
Departament d'Economia i Organització d'Empreses, Facultat d'Economia i Empresa,
Universitat de Barcelona, Avda. Diagonal, 690, 08034 Barcelona, Spain
e-mail: farizaa@ub.edu; santiago.forgas@ub.edu

R. Palau-Saumell
Institut Quimic de Sarrià, IQS School of Management, Universitat Ramon Liull,
Via Augusta, 390, 08017 Barcelona, Spain
e-mail: ramon.palau@iqs.url.edu

9.1 Introduction

The construction of the European Higher Education Area (EHEA) has brought with it several profound changes in the university environment and the process of design, evaluation and implementation of new curricula. The reshaping of degree courses, the introduction of a new credit accounting system focused on student workload (ECTS, European Credit Transfer System) and skills learning methodologies are three central features of this new educational paradigm. In fact, Spanish universities have been very careful in defining the competencies that students must achieve within the new degrees and postgraduate courses. However, they have paid less attention to the question of how these competencies should be measured.

In many cases, student skills cannot be evaluated by the traditional assessment methods (Makatsoris 2009). A recent analysis of several degree syllabuses in Spain highlighted the deficiencies of these traditional methods (Mano-González and Moro-Cabero 2009). In general, the process of competency assessment has been somewhat neglected in Spanish higher education.

The present study addresses this issue by exploring the implementation of a tool for assessing competencies. Broad competencies were assessed using the methodology of the Evolute project, developed by the Tampere University of Technology in Finland (Kantola 2005, 2009; Kantola et al. 2005; Vanharanta 2005). This is an ICT-based digital platform designed for the self-assessment of personal and social competencies, and it uses different models of competencies for a range of student profiles.[1] Here we chose the application known as *Cranioid–Innovators' competencies*, due to its compatibility with both the objectives of the syllabus and the broad competencies to be achieved by students in the Master's degree under consideration, i.e. *Creating and Managing Innovative Technology-Based Companies*.[2]

At the level of teaching, the *Cranioid* tool enables educators to assess an individual student's competencies in specific areas of interest, the results being produced immediately. The analysis is performed automatically by the system (Makatsoris 2009) and provides teachers with additional information about the effects of their input on student competencies, doing so at a negligible cost (in terms of time and effort). It also complements other assessment instruments or methods

---

[1] The authors of this research collaborate with the G•IDEA, a consolidated teaching innovation group, which has a large previous experience in implementing Evolute tools in different subjects in the area of management (see http://www.ub.edu/gidea).

[2] The aim of this Master's programme is to develop a reference platform capable of providing high-level training, skills and qualifications for entrepreneurs in technology-based companies and, in general, for the managers of innovative firms. The Master's is designed such that students acquire the competencies required to satisfactorily achieve the following objectives: (a) To carry out processes related to the creation of companies, especially those which are technology-based; (b) To manage technology-based companies from start-up through to consolidation; (c) To design and successfully implement R + D projects and management plans within the company; and (d) To have in-depth knowledge of the scientific and technological context, and of the key players within it, in order to develop cooperative and technology-transfer agreements with them.

that teachers might use to evaluate the outcomes of competency-based teaching/learning. At the individual level the *Cranioid* application should be considered as a tool for students' personal development, since it enables them to identify their strong and weak points and to develop personal strategies for improvement that can have an impact on their innovative profile and academic performance. Finally, at the institutional level the tool provides an opportunity for continuous improvement, since it can detect trends in the training needs of new students and help to foster the development of the competencies required by tailoring the academic programme accordingly.

This latter aspect is important in the context of Master's degrees, whose close links with professional careers mean that particular attention is paid to quality, not only by universities or the certification and accreditation agencies, but also by various key players in the business community. Among other things this has led to an increasing emphasis being placed on the competencies required for the professional career towards which the training and qualifications are geared.

Being able to match training to the needs of the labour market is important not only for those who are charged with designing academic programmes in different fields, but also for educators who wish to become more efficient in their teaching activity. In order to achieve such a match it is necessary to determine the initial level of students' competencies at the start of a given academic programme, compare this with what is required by the career they are seeking, and tailor the teaching/learning process accordingly. However, these skills and competencies are not readily captured through traditional assessment methods (Makatsoris 2009), and their analysis becomes even more difficult in the context of new postgraduate courses, due to the wide range of backgrounds from which students come. In this context the use of ICT-based tools provides a cost-effective and quick way of assessing the competencies of individual students and of monitoring them throughout the course.

The overall aim of this chapter is to increase our understanding of ways of assessing competencies and illustrate how these can benefit the university community. More specifically, the objectives are threefold: Firstly, validating methods of assessment that can help teaching staff to analyse and evaluate the acquisition and mastery of competencies among their students. Secondly, examining the utility of self-assessment of competencies and the use of an ICT-based tool for providing feedback about students' progress. Thirdly, determining the extent to which the tool *Cranioid* provides useful information for the quality management of Master's programmes.

This chapter describes our experience of applying the digital platform Evolute and, specifically, the tool *Cranioid* in order to evaluate broad competencies among students enrolled in the Master's programme *Creating and Managing Innovative Technology-Based Companies*. The analysis was carried out in September of 2010, in the very beginning of the course, the aim being to assess the extent to which the course content matched the needs of students and, where necessary, to make any improvements required.

9.2 Theoretical Framework: The Literature on Competencies

The term 'competency' has taken on great importance within the current educational paradigm, although there seems to be no consensus over its definition. This is perhaps unsurprising given the wide range of fields involved and the diversity of approaches used in the study of competencies (Sultana 2009). Nevertheless, notable efforts have been made to describe and clarify the different approaches to the concept, good examples being the work of Winterton et al. (2005), Delamare Le Deist and Winterton (2005), and Mulder et al. (2007). These and other studies point out that a distinction has traditionally been made between three main approaches: the behavioural, the functional and the holistic.

The behavioural approach, as proposed by McClelland (1998), is based on the evaluation of demonstrable and observable behaviour. Authors who adopt this perspective consider competencies as those attributes of a person which are related to the effective execution of a task, and to performance that is notably better than that of other individuals carrying out the same activity (Delamare Le Deist and Winterton 2005; Spencer and Spencer 1993; White 1959). Consequently, it is an approach that focuses on those personal attributes which are readily applicable to other work contexts.

The functional approach is given particular emphasis in the United Kingdom, due to the government's efforts to implement a nationally harmonized competency-based system of training in the workplace. In the functional approach, competency refers to those attributes that enable a set of tasks to be successfully carried out (functions that are more or less permanent), these taking precedence over the personal attributes of the individual who performs the task (Blanco-Prieto 2007). Therefore, this approach centres on work outcomes, in accordance with a number of parameters that have previously been established in relation to a specific activity.

The holistic approach seeks to integrate the above two perspectives. Thus, it considers competencies as those attributes required to perform a task in accordance with a set of specified parameters. In sum, it links the analysis of individual attributes (the behavioural approach) with the study of the characteristics needed in a given workplace (the functional approach). This approach is traditionally associated with the system of training used in France and Germany.

The holistic approach provides the conceptual framework of competency adopted in the present study, drawing upon the definition of Bikfalvi et al. (2007), who state that 'competencies refer to the attributes, knowledge, skills, experience and values that an individual needs to carry out his/her tasks'. This definition links the general attribute approach with the context in which such attributes are put into practice.

9.3 Models of Competencies

A model of competencies is a descriptive tool that serves to identify the skills, knowledge and personal attributes required to achieve effectively a set of objectives, whether in terms of student learning or workers' ability to fulfil their role within an

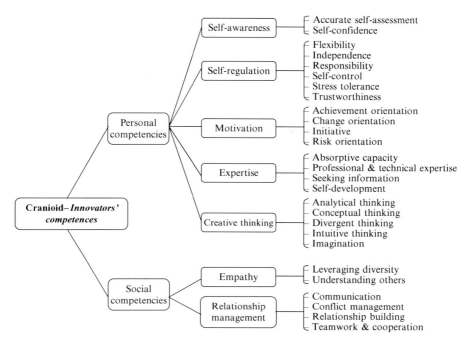

Fig. 9.1 CRANIOID Competencies' model — Innovators' competencies (Reproduced from Jussila 2007)

organization. In other words, it is a description of the competencies needed to function in a specific job or workplace (Ennis 2008; Gangani et al. 2006; Lucia and Lepsinger 1999) and serves to evaluate individual competencies in relation to a given profile (Zwell 2000). These competencies are often presented in the form of hierarchical and categorized maps (Sandwith 1993).

In the present study the assessment of competencies in relation to innovative profiles was based on the tool known as *Cranioid–Innovators' competencies*, which is described in detail by Jussila (2007). This model is shown in Fig. 9.1.

9.4 Methodology

As mentioned before, to carry out the competency evaluation in the Master's programme *Creating and Managing Innovative Technology-Based Companies* we chose a tool named *Cranioid* developed by the Tampere University of Technology (Finland). This University, as part of the project known as Evolute, has developed a new method and new tools for assessing competencies.

The various applications offered by Evolute have been designed to evaluate the desirable competencies in a range of professional roles (for example, project managers or those in charge of health and safety at work) and organizational processes (knowledge creation, innovative culture, managing the value chain, etc.). It should be noted that these applications are distinct and tailored to each professional role and organizational process. One of such applications is *Cranioid–Innovators' competencies*, an ICT-based tool that enables the self-assessment of an individual's innovative skills.

The methodology followed in this chapter to apply the *Cranioid* tool has been adapted by Bikfalvi et al. (2007) and Makatsoris (2009) for similar projects. Thus, it can be broken down into three stages: a pre-evaluation, evaluation and post-evaluation stages.

In the pre-evaluation stage, students are provided with information and documentation about the objectives, content and functioning of the tool. They are also given all the necessary instructions to ensure they can use the tool successfully, along with the username and password required to access the system.

The evaluation stage of the *Cranioid* tool is based on the indirect self-assessment of broad competencies. Thus, students are asked to respond to a series of statements related to their daily work, but in such a way that their impression is that they are assessing their attitudes, perceptions and feelings, etc. rather than their performance. For each statement they are asked to identify their current level of competency and indicate the level they would like to achieve. Statements are graded using a fuzzy scale, with labels such as always, often, sometimes or never. The difference between the two levels (current and desired) is referred to as the creative tension, on the basis of which it is possible to identify competencies for which the student perceives the need to learn. In other words, one can identify those areas on which further training could usefully be focused.

The *Cranioid* questionnaire contains 103 items relating to daily work activities. The scores derived from the responses given, for both the current and desired levels, provide an immediate evaluation of 27 broad competencies (personal and social) (see Fig. 9.1).

After completing the self-evaluation, we carry out the post-evaluation stage, which consists of giving the participants a post-evaluation questionnaire in order to gather information about how they perceived various aspects such as the importance of the competencies assessed, the subjective validity of the tool, and their opinion about the extent to which their studies help them to develop their competencies.

The competency evaluation and the *Cranioid* application was administered at the start of the 2010/2011 academic year to 20 students, who participated voluntarily in the project, enrolled in the Master's programme *Creating and Managing Innovative Technology-Based Companies* held in the Faculty of Economics and Business of the University of Barcelona. As regards the profile of these students, 50 % were male, 50 % were Spanish (the rest were from different foreign countries), 62 % were between 25 and 30 years old, and 55 % had prior innovation trainings.

9.5 Results

The results for the evaluation of the broad competencies using the *Cranioid* tool according to the innovative profile of students are shown in Fig. 9.2. The aggregate results for the 27 competencies considered by the model are ordered by creative tension. This form of presentation is that used by the Evolute platform to indicate the current level of competencies (light grey bars), the desired levels (dark grey bars) and the creative tension (the distance between the two levels).

It can be seen that the competencies with the greatest creative tension are, in this order: Self-control, Absorptive capacity, Stress tolerance, Communication and Change orientation. It is on these five competencies that students believe they have to improve the most, since it is here that there is the greatest distance between the current and desired levels of competency.

Conversely, the competencies on which students regard themselves as well-prepared, i.e. those with the least creative tension, are, in this order: Risk

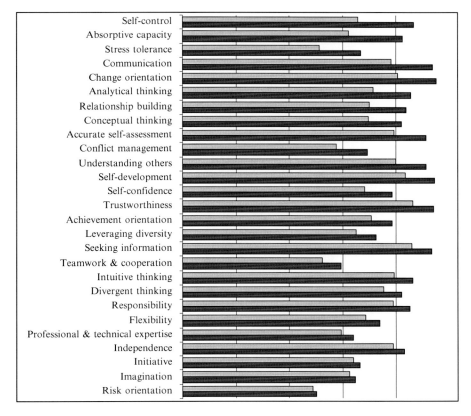

Fig. 9.2 Competencies of the Master's programme students as a whole (ordered by creative tension)

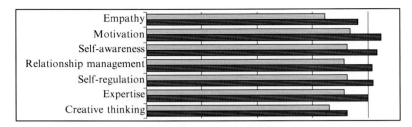

Fig. 9.3 Groups of competencies for the Master's programme students as a whole (ordered by creative tension)

Fig. 9.4 The two main groups of competencies for the Master's programme students as a whole (ordered by creative tension)

orientation, Imagination, Initiative, Independence and Professional and technical expertise. These competencies can therefore be considered as those on which students feel better equipped.

Figure 9.3 presents the competencies of the model organized into seven groups: Empathy, Motivation, Self-awareness, Relationship management, Self-regulation, Expertise and Creative thinking. Of these, the group in which students show the greatest creative tension, and therefore perceive as a priority area with the most scope for improvement, is Empathy. By contrast, the group with the lowest creative tension, corresponding to the competencies on which the students regard themselves as better equipped, is Creative thinking.

As regards the two main groups of competencies (personal and social), Fig. 9.4 shows that the perceived difference between students' current and desired level of competency is greater for social than for personal competencies.

Finally, Table 9.1 shows results, measured on a 7-point Likert scale, of students' perceptions regarding the importance of the competencies assessed, the validity of the *Cranioid* tool for evaluating these competencies, and their opinions about the extent to which their studies help them to develop their competency as regards entrepreneurship and innovativeness.

As regards the evaluation of each of the seven competency groups, it can be seen in Table 9.1 that students ascribe considerable importance to the social and personal competencies described by the model, the scores given being above 5.75 out of 7. Also the results obtained from the evaluation of each of the seven competency groups illustrate that students regard the tool as an adequate and valid measure of their competencies, with scores out of 7 being 5.3 or higher. Finally, the students believe that the Master's programme makes a considerable contribution to the development of their broad competencies. The competency which they regarded as

9 Exploring the Use of an ICT-Based Tool for Assessing Competencies…

Table 9.1 Students' evaluation of broad competencies and the *Cranioid* tool

	Groups of competencies	Mean score on a scale of 1–7
Importance to the student of the social and personal competencies	Motivation	6.5
	Self-awareness	6.15
	Self-regulation	6
	Relationship management	6
	Creative thinking	5.9
	Expertise	5.85
	Empathy	5.75
Students' evaluation regarding the suitability of the tool for assessing broad competencies	Motivation	5.95
	Empathy	5.8
	Self-regulation	5.75
	Self-awareness	5.7
	Relationship management	5.7
	Creative thinking	5.6
	Expertise	5.3
Students' evaluation regarding the contribution of the Master's programme to the development of broad competencies	Relationship management	5.8
	Expertise	5.35
	Creative thinking	5.35
	Motivation	4.9
	Empathy	4.45
	Self-awareness	4.35
	Self-regulation	4.25

being most developed was Relationship management (score of 5.8), and even the competency which they felt was least influenced by their studies, i.e. Self-regulation, still achieved a high score (4.25).

All these results, together with the others obtained during the project described in this chapter, provide valuable information that can be used to develop strategies for improving the quality of the University of Barcelona's Master's programme *Creating and Managing Innovative Technology-Based Companies*.

9.6 Conclusions

This chapter has presented the results obtained with the *Cranioid* tool for assessing cross-disciplinary skills in relation to the innovative profile of students on the Official Master's Programme *Creating and Managing Innovative Technology-Based Companies* at the University of Barcelona at the beginning of the course. The results suggest the skills that students felt they needed to improve most (the skills with the largest gap between the current and the desired levels) and the skills that students felt they mastered, and so that the Master's programme does not need to prioritize.

Consequently, tools such as the *Cranioid* can help university managers in designing the academic programmes as it allows assessing the initial students' competence level embarking on academic programmes and to compare it with the level required for their future professional development. An efficient assessment system as this is needed to enable managers to develop teaching–learning processes tailored to students' needs. Hence, this kind of self-assessment benefits the three parties involved: students, university managers and organizations, and should be applied along the students curricula as a transversal project and adapt the programs to achieve graduate and postgraduate students with higher levels of social and personal competences, as demanded by the labour market.

References

Bikfalvi A, Llach-Pages J, Kantola J, Marques-Gou P, Mancebo-Fernandez N (2007) Complementing education with competency development: an ICT-based application. Int J Manag Educ 1(3):231–250
Blanco-Prieto A (2007) Trabajadores competentes. Introducción y reflexiones sobre la gestión de recursos humanos por competencias. ESIC Editorial, Madrid
Delamare Le Deist F, Winterton J (2005) What is competency? Hum Resour Dev Int 8(1):27–46
Ennis MR (2008) Competency models: a review of the literature and the role of the Employment and Training Administration (ETA), ETA Research Publication Database. http://www.careeronestop.org/competencymodel/info_documents/OPDRLiteratureReview.pdf. Accessed 15 Sept 2013
Gangani N, McLean GN, Braden RA (2006) A competency-based human resource development strategy. Perform Improv Q 19(1):127–139
Jussila J (2007) Innovation competence. Màster of science thesis, Tampere University of Technology at Pori, Tampere
Kantola J (2005) Ingenious management. Doctoral thesis, Tampere University of Technology at Pori, Tampere
Kantola J (2009) Ontology-based resource management. Hum Factors Ergon Manuf Serv Ind 19(6):515–527
Kantola J, Vanharanta H, Karwowski W (2005) The Evolute system: a co-evolutionary human resource development methodology. In: Karwowski W (ed) International encyclopedia of ergonomics and human factors. CRC, Boca Raton, pp 2894–2900
Lucia AD, Lepsinger R (1999) The art and science of competency models. Jossey-Bass/Pfeiffer, San Francisco
Makatsoris C (2009) An information and communication technologies-based framework for enhancing project management education through competency assessment and development. Hum Factors Ergon Manuf 19(6):544–567
Mano-González M, Moro-Cabero M (2009) L'avaluació per competències: proposta d'un sistema de mesura per al grau d'Informació i Documentació. Textos universitaris de biblioteconomia i documentació, 23. http://www.ub.edu/bid/23/delamano1.htm. Accessed 12 Oct 2013
McClelland DC (1998) Identifying competencies with behavioral event interviews. Psychol Sci 9(5):331–339
Mulder M, Weigel T, Collins K (2007) The concept of competency in the development of vocational education and training in selected EU member status: a critical analysis. J Vocat Educ Train 59(1):67–88
Sandwith P (1993) A hierarchy of management training requirements: the competency domain model. Public Pers Manag 22(1):43–62

Spencer L, Spencer S (1993) Competency at work: a model for superior performance. Wiley, New York

Sultana RG (2009) Competency and competency frameworks in career guidance: complex and contested concepts. Int J Educ Vocat Guid 9(1):15–30

Vanharanta H (2005) Plenary at HCI International Conference 2005, Las Vegas, Nevada, 22–27 July 2005

White R (1959) Motivation reconsidered: the concept of competency. Psychol Rev 66:279–333

Winterton J, Delamare Le Deist F, Stringfellow E (2005) Typology of knowledge, skills and competencies: clarification of the concept and prototype (Panorama Series, 1397). Office for Official Publications of the European Communities, Luxembourg

Zwell M (2000) Creating a culture of competency. Wiley, New York

Chapter 10
A Proposal for Using Lego Serious Play in Education

Jose O. Montesa-Andres, Fernando J. Garrigós-Simón, and Yeamduan Narangajavana

Abstract The dynamics of our society is forcing change in the education system. The knowledge students had to learn remained stable for long periods. And even when that knowledge changed the learning frameworks remained. Nowadays, the environment, what we know about any subject, and the stability of our knowledge are constantly changing. This paper presents an attempt to find new learning methods, with the objective of creating a process where students learn current models and frames, while preparing them for change. We have worked with Lego© Serious Play© over 12 months and it provides an alternative model of the way students learn and the work of teachers. In this new process, the teacher becomes a facilitator and consultant who prepares the learning journey and leads the process.

10.1 Introduction

As teachers, our starting point is usually near the Newtonian paradigm, where we presume an ordered universe in our subject, and attempt to introduce this order into our students' brains. We know that this world is simply our perception, in fact the perception shared by a group of people (academics) who spend their time trying to perceive the subject and provide a coherent model of what we see. But our students must be prepared for something different, according to Watkins et al. (2011:15): "For past generations the Newtonian paradigm fitted nicely into the comfort zone for most people. It is still hard for most of us to wrap our brains around such

---

J.O. Montesa-Andres (✉) • F.J. Garrigós-Simón
Departamento de Organización de Empresas, Universitat Politècnica de València,
Camino de Vera, s/n, 46022 Valencia, Spain
e-mail: jomontes@omp.upv.es; fergars3@doe.upv.es

Y. Narangajavana
Business School, Walailak University, 222 Thaiburi, Thasala District,
Nakhon Si Thammarat, 80160, Thailand
e-mail: nu_awn@hotmail.com

questions as: 'Is order essential to the structure of the universe or is it simply a product of human perception?'." If order is indeed simply a product of human perception, students must perceive this order, as the state of the art, and as a serious model before they can understand the subject being taught.

Subjects we teach may remain unaltered during our students' lifetimes. We can look at previous changes in a subject, and imagine how that knowledge will change in the future. The difficulty lies in trying to envision radical changes.

In view of the above, teachers therefore face a complex situation. With previous paradigms, students had to learn the order created in a subject. But nowadays, we need to prepare our students for more flexible situations, although the time available for each subject remains the same. We now have a clearer understanding of disruptive science and the problems the people involved in scientific breakthroughs had with their teachers when they were young. We also know that people who do not accept previous perceptions (paradigms) of a subject have fewer problems addressing new views.

Students need to be provided with first-hand experiences, make their own reflections, and then be shown the current knowledge. They must also be active in working to understand their experiences and draw their own conclusions.

Our work focuses on knowledge management and learning organizations, and so we approach the learning process from this point of view. Organizations are the context in which our students are likely to work and indeed, where they will learn in the future.

10.2 Theoretical Framework: Knowledge Management and Learning Organizations

According to Hicks (1999), there are some formal learning situations, where individuals consciously "learn" and "study." However, at other times learning is a spontaneous process (without any necessary deliberations or assessments) or occurs at many levels and in many ways. Information or skills may be imparted quite explicitly and at the same time the values and attitudes of the trainer will also be implicitly communicated, or we may be learning "incidentally" at times, as we acquire, process and remember information automatically.

According to March and Simon (1958), account must also be taken of the fact that people cannot heed and listen to everything in the environment, as the sensorial system has various physical limits that make our attention and perception selective. The way we categorize and organize information is based on a wide variety of factors, including the present situation, our mood and emotional state and also our previous experiences of the same or similar event. In addition, humans make a number of inferences that, if true enable us to save time and speed up the process, they also lead to distortions and inadequacies. This fact influences students' conceptions of reality and also their behaviors in the classroom.

In order to understand the learning process, we have to focus on knowledge itself and ways to improve it. In this vein, Polanyi (1966) established the difference between tacit knowledge and explicit knowledge, a distinction that has been used broadly by professionals and researchers in areas such as knowledge management (Herschel et al. 2001:107).

Explicit knowledge is clearly formulated or defined, easily expressed without ambiguity or vagueness and codified and stored in databases (Bollinger and Smith 2001:9). This knowledge can be coded in writing or symbols. However, only a small part of our knowledge is explicit: we know more than we can tell (Polanyi 1966:4).

Tacit knowledge is unarticulated knowledge in people's minds and it is often difficult to describe and transfer (Bollinger and Smith 2001:9). It is the knowledge we all feel we understand, but is ultimately difficult to articulate clearly (Polanyi 1966). Polanyi covers the aspects of knowledge that are hidden and impossible to articulate (Gómez and Jones 2000:697).

According to Hall (2001), tacit knowledge is subjective and known by the individuals themselves, it can be even partially unconscious as in the case of habits and skills. In contrast, explicit knowledge is codified, objective, often annotated and sharable and always flows from human relations. This distinction is crucial because of the "transferability" and "appropriability" of explicit knowledge as opposed to tacit knowledge (Grant 1996); and it is essential for understanding the importance of other ways of learning, apart from the traditional focus on the oral transmission of information in schools.

In addition to this distinction, Nonaka and his co-researchers describe two possible dimensions of tacit knowledge (Kidd 2001:117). The first is technical "know-how." The second is cognitive, comprising beliefs and mental models developed over the years whose schemes are difficult to change because often we "take them for granted." Given these differences, Nonaka and Takeuchi (1995) provide a model that refers to "the various stages in the dynamic spiral of learning" (Kidd 2001:117).

According to Nonaka and Takeuchi (1995:225), knowledge conversion among members of any organization occurs in four stages:

1. Socialization (from tacit to tacit knowledge), or the sharing of knowledge over time. This stage develops through the fact of being together and sharing experiences over time, rather than through verbal and written exchanges.
2. "Outsourcing" (from tacit to explicit knowledge). This stage requires the expression of tacit knowledge through metaphors, analogies or narratives, means used by individuals to integrate into a group's mental world.
3. Combination (from explicit to explicit knowledge). In this third stage Nonaka and Takeuchi talk about communication and dissemination. This stage involves three steps: collection of explicit knowledge, external dissemination of this knowledge and the publication of new material to make it more useful.
4. Finally, the fourth stage is one of "internalization" or conversion of explicit knowledge into tacit knowledge by identifying the self knowledge needed to work in the organization. This stage includes training programs and simulations embedded in learning through action.

Although Nonaka and Takeuchi attempt to explain how knowledge emerges and is transformed in organizations and we focus only on education in the classroom, we think that these approaches serve to reveal the steps that an individual can take to obtain knowledge, and examine aspects such as the fact that accumulations of information are of little value: only information which is actively processed in an individual's mind through a process of reflection, clarification and learning can be useful.

A focus on the individual's external environment (in this case the situation in the classroom) rather than only on their skills and capabilities can help to improve the educational process. Although the learning process includes aspects of private life or life outside the classroom and individuals' skills and capabilities, we should not forget that many of the aspects that influence learning are mediated and to some extent enhanced by the mechanisms of obtaining knowledge within the classroom, so attention to these aspects is crucial. According to Hicks (1999:346–347), many internal (perception, memory, motivation, attitudes, ability level, emotions) and external factors (relationships, rewards and punishments, environment, context, methods such as facilities or tutors, etc.) constantly affect each other in the process of learning.

In this frame the school as a learning organization is key for developing knowledge, and improving learning itself.

In the 1970s, some authors popularize the concept of the learning organization. This frame was developed with the work of Argyris and Schön (1974), Senge (1990), or Pedler et al. (1991). However, the concept was not new, since in the 1960s, Cyert and March (1963) devoted a section in their book to "organizational learning," talking about adapter behavior over time, using individual members as a tool (Cyert and March 1963:172).

However, the focus of learning organization places more emphasis on the role of the organization as a vehicle for learning. According to Argyris, each individual has a potential that can be intensified or reduced depending on how the organization is managed, thereby highlighting the importance of organizations in their members' personal development.

There are many definitions of a learning organization. For instance Garvin (1993) described it as an organization that is skilled at creating, acquiring, and transferring knowledge and at modifying its behavior to reflect new knowledge and insights. These skills include problem solving, learning from past experiences, experimenting with newly learned techniques and assumptions and managing knowledge within the organization. Pedler et al. (1991) provide one of the most commonly used definitions of a learning company as an organization that facilitates learning in all its members and continuously transforms itself and its context.

Another important contribution is from Senge (1990) and Senge et al. (1999) who proposes the "learning organization" as a practical model. He argues that a learning organization has the ability for both generative learning (i.e., active) and adapter learning (i.e., passive). According to Senge (1990:12–13), a learning organization is a place where people are continually discovering how they create their reality and how they can change. Senge (1990) and Senge et al. (1999) also emphasizes five disciplines required for building learning organizations:

(a) Personal mastery: involves formulating a coherent picture of a personal vision (the results people most desire to gain as individuals), taking into account a realistic assessment of the current state of their personal realities.
(b) Mental models: images, assumptions and stories we carry in our minds about ourselves, other people, institutions and all aspects of the world. They are

important as they can distort our vision, and also our behaviors. These models are tacit and invisible.
(c) Shared vision: stresses the relevance of a mutual purpose. The creation of a shared vision helps to create a sense of belonging and consequently, commitment. Teachers need time, attention and strategy to develop this discipline.
(d) Team learning: a discipline of group interaction, which concentrates on a group's collective potential. People work well when they allow others to work well. There is an alignment and they function as a whole. Teams must transform their collective thinking, through techniques like dialogue and skillful discussion.
(e) System thinking: the ability to approach the world with a wide-angle lens, to see how our actions relate to other areas of the same activity; focusing on feedback loop behavior and the complex characteristics of a system.

10.3 Lego© Serious Play© Process

The term "Serious Play" is used with different meanings, always far removed from leisure and near to business, industry or war, as Roger Smith proposes in INTSEC 2009 (tr. 4/81). The most general definition we found was: "games that do not have entertainment, enjoyment or fun as their primary purpose" (Michael and Chen 2005). Some authors include serious games as a subset of video games, as Minhua Ma et al. (2011:9) propose in "Innovations in Serious Games for Future Learning," when they write: "The recent emergence of serious games as a branch of video games …"

"Lego Serious Play" (LSP) falls within Michel and Chen's definition, but is closer to face-to-face interaction between people and physical objects than videogames.

According to Rasmunssen in "The Science of LEGO SERIOUS PLAY," "SERIOUS PLAY is a concept developed over several years by Executive Discovery, a member of the LEGO Group. It emerged out of the research and experience of a number of academics and practitioners searching for more effective ways to meet the increasingly complex and challenging demands of the business world." This definition contextualizes the tool, but in order to understand the tool, Rasmunssen clarifies "what" LSP delivers to users: "SERIOUS PLAY is our name for the process we have developed to bring the creativity, the exuberance, and the inspiration of play to the serious concerns of adults in the business world." Both definitions are obviously commercial messages, but we (along with other universities, companies and governments) are interested in the fact that this tool is used to improve companies, as reported in the "White Paper on LEGO® SERIOUS PLAY® a state of the art of its applications in Europe."

We start by analyzing LSP in order to understand and break it down into its different components, in order to use them in the learning process. We experienced LSP in several sessions provided by an LSP facilitator to observe the process and its dynamics.

These LSP sessions appear to be an evolution of the exercises proposed by Michalko in "Thinkertoys", and similar to the "Gamestorming" proposed by Gray et al.

According to "Gamestorming" "successful creative people tend to employ simple strategies and practices to get where they want to go," and call them games.

From the management point of view, LSP is reminiscent of the process proposed in "The Dance of Change" by Peter Senge and of the concepts proposed in "A Positive Revolution in Change: Appreciative Inquiry" by David L. Cooperrider and Diana Whitney.

According to Frick et al.'s simple definition "(LSP) is a facilitated workshop where participants respond to tasks by building symbolic and metaphorical models with LEGO bricks and present them to the other participants."

LSP proposes two levels of action, a basic core level and the workshop process level.

The workshop process addresses a route defined by the facilitator and some champions in the company that people participating in the workshop must follow.

The route is similar to what Gamestorming calls the "game of business" where you identify where you are and where you want to go. If the goal is clear and unambiguous, the idea is to go from the starting point to the goal crossing a set of pre-established points, and step by step reach that goal by including all the participants' points of view. As Gamestorming addresses innovation, the goals are usually ambiguous, uncertain, and volatile. The "game of business" can be planned like any project, but the facilitator must be aware of new directions and allow the team to take them. The problem for the facilitator is to determine if the chosen way will achieve the goal (generally a broad range of points are accepted as the goal). The facilitator is an important actor, as Gamestorming notes: "keep in mind that you may have more experience navigating complex challenge spaces than some of the other people in the room. You may have a better sense of how far along you are than they do. If you are the captain of the ship, it may make people nervous if you express too much doubt."

In the introduction, LSP assigns the facilitator with a different role, "Building upon the inclusive and participatory nature of the LEGO System, LEGO® SERIOUS PLAY® rejects the idea that external 'experts' must be brought in to identify problems, and to propose solutions; on the contrary, LEGO® SERIOUS PLAY® begins with the assumption that the answers are 'already in the room'." Therefore the LSP facilitator is similar to the Appreciative Inquiry facilitator in Watkins' proposal where "the [Organization Development] OD Consultant facilitates the process so the role of consultant is almost invisible."

The LSP core process is the process to be followed with each question and is structured as follows (Lego Serious Play Methodology, 7):

1. The first step of the ideal learning spiral is to help people connect to what they are going to explore, and to understand the context and meaning of what they are about to learn more about.
2. The second step is to involve people in a process where they create a product connected to the targets of exploration, involving their own knowledge and reflections as well as their own creative skills—and their own hands.
3. The third step is to help people reflect on what they have created and look deeper into their own reflections about their own product, in order to become aware of what their explorations have brought them, and in order to gain more insights.

4. The fourth step is that people get a chance to connect their newly gained knowledge to new explorations they would want to pursue.

10.4 Proposal

We apply an adaptation of LSP in the classroom. Fig. 10.1 shows the students' initial level of competence in the subject, different for each student, due to each student's previous experiences.

In Fig. 10.1, the knowledge to be taught in a session is shaped by the learning objectives and the transversal competences to be addressed.

We must identify the student's knowledge and ask questions related to their prior knowledge, so they can play and talk around these concepts, individually and in the learning group. We represent as "student X prior knowledge" the knowledge each student has. This area is a comfort area for the students, in this area we know that if you try to teach by telling, students with enough knowledge will be bored. But if you ask them, they are happy and involved in the answer. Questions must be created to address this involvement. Based on Nonaka's model, we try to transform student's tacit knowledge into explicit knowledge by modeling it with Lego metaphors. We activate this process in the second step of the LSP core process. Students are asked to create a metaphor for the item with LEGO bricks, and then develop a story to share their points of view with the others.

Students usually listen to each other's story, some because they have knowledge and they want to tell their stories in a proper manner, while others recognize their ignorance and learn by means of these stories. Fig. 10.1 shows that students overlap and can be talking about things connecting the knowledge. In this situation, students learn sharable knowledge by peer learning. Here, the teacher must be ready to clarify what has been said in contrast to LSP where the facilitator did not add new information.

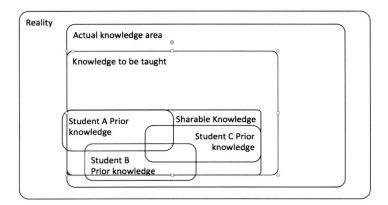

Fig. 10.1 Knowledge to be taught in a learning process

The next step is when students combine their knowledge, creating a landscape of what they are talking about (the sharable area is completed). Again the teacher takes the opportunity to order their knowledge. The teacher usually has a landscape model (a Business Model Canvas, a Conceptual map, or a Mind map) and students do not usually question the model. At this stage, students put their creations on a surface, or just parts of their creations, because they believe that other students express a concept in a better way; they are free to select as a team the items to represent the acquired knowledge. More than that, they feel comfortable in this atmosphere of collaboration and they talk about the model. As the teacher proposes the framework for the LEGOs, sometimes students start looking at certain "empty spaces" in the landscape, and they expect something to cover them. This anticipation activates questions about the subject they can ask to improve their own knowledge and other students' knowledge too. With the landscape the teacher can ask questions and students can answer easily due to the items on the table, recalling the concepts and relations modeled as strings or lines connecting the concepts. Although the process seems to be clearly specified, the teacher needs extra material and other types of activities in order to address the covered area because some students want to work more deeply with certain concepts.

Students usually enjoy these learning processes; they play and feel free to express their points of view. When asked about the experience, curiously their replies are similar to the responses when LSP is used in industry.

Students socialize their knowledge and themselves in the group, generating a high level of satisfaction. Some students ask for this type of activities at the beginning of the course in order to get to know the other students. Fellowship increases.

When you use these techniques students use their hands (constructing with Lego©), become creative, make up and tell stories, open their minds to the question more freely, they feel part of a team, and if the final landscape is modeled as a system, they gain a systemic view of the knowledge. When you propose a way of completing the knowledge they are ready to take it on board.

References

Argyris C, Schön D (1974) Theory in practice. Jossey Bass, San Francisco
Bollinger AS, Smith R (2001) Managing organizational knowledge as a strategic asset. J Knowl Manag 5(1):8–18
Cyert RM, March JG (1963) A behavioral theory of the firm, 2nd edn. Prentice-Hall, New York. de 1992, reprint in 1996. Blackwell, Cambridge
Garvin DA (1993) Building a learning organization. Harv Bus Rev 71(4):78–91
Gómez PY, Jones BC (2000) Conventions: an interpretation of deep structure in organizations. Organ Sci 11(6):696–708
Grant RM (1996) Toward a knowledge-based theory of the firm. Strateg Manag J 17:109–122
Hall BP (2001) Values development and learning organizations. J Knowl Manag 5(1):19–32
Herschel RT, Nemati H, Steiger D (2001) Tacit to explicit knowledge conversion: knowledge exchange protocols. J Knowl Manag 5(1):107–116

Hicks L (1999) The nature of learning. In: Mullins LJ (ed) Management and organizational behaviour, 5th edn. Pitman, London, pp 344–375. Financial Times

Kidd JB (2001) Discovering inter-cultural perceptual differences in MNEs. J Manag Psychol 16(2):106–126

Ma M, Oikonomou A, Jain LC (2011) Serious games and edutainment applications. Springer, Berlin

March JG, Simon HA (1958) Organizations. New York: Wiley

Michael D, Chen S (2005) Serious games: games that educate, train, and inform, 1st edn. Course Technology PTR, USA. In "Origins of Serious Games"

Nonaka I, Takeuchi H (1995) The knowledge-creating company. Oxford University Press, Oxford

Pedler M, Burgoyne J, Boydell T (1991) The learning company: a strategy for sustainable development. McGraw-Hill, London

Polanyi M (1966) The tacit dimension. Routledge & Kegan Paul, London

Senge P (1990) The fifth discipline, the art and practice of the learning organisation. Random House, London

Senge P, Kleiner A, Roberts C, Ross R, Roth G, Smith B (1999) The dance of change: the challenges of sustaining momentum in learning organizations. A fifth discipline resource. Nicholas Brealey, London

Watkins JM, Mohr BJ, Ralph K (2011) Appreciative inquiry: change at the speed of imagination, 2nd edn. Pfeiffer, San Francisco

Chapter 11
Applying Teamwork Competence in a Company Course

Teresa Barbera Ribera, Marta Palmer Gato, José Miguel Albarracín Guillem, and Carlos M. Dema Pérez

Abstract This chapter describes the experience of developing team work skills in a practical module. This experience took place during a course given to workers in a Valencian company. All the skills are easier to apply and develop in smaller groups. During this course the attention given to the students was increased in the following basic aspects: utilization of cases and team work, personal tutorials and attention. The results obtained are seen after the realization of the experiment, with post experience evaluation undertaken by the students.

11.1 Introduction

This methodological innovation attempts to encourage collaborative learning, autonomy to learn, and the development of distinct styles of learning within the student body. The traditional teaching style emphasises theory and reflection. The methodological renovation promotes student participation in learning as well as collaboration with fellow students, favouring the integral development of the students, including the personal dimension, contact with reality and social projection, all in an integrated way (Villardón and Yániz 2003).

The European Higher Education Space (EEES) promotes a theory based upon the supposition that efficient learning will only occur when the actual student assumes responsibility for the organization and development of their academic work (De Miguel Díaz 2006). In Europe it is impossible to speak of only one teaching method, instead one must speak of a diversity of approaches that point towards

T.B. Ribera • M.P. Gato • J.M.A. Guillem (✉) • C.M.D. Pérez
Departamento de Organización de Empresas, Universitat Politècnica de València,
Camino de Vera, s/n 46022, Valencia, Spain
e-mail: mabarri@upvnet.upv.es; marpalga@doe.upv.es; jmalbarr@doe.upv.es;
jmalbarr@omp.upv.es; cmdema@omp.upv.es

greater involvement of the student in their learning (MEC 2006). But this process did not simply suppose an adjustment of procedures and criteria at the European level, but also puts forward a profound change in the educational paradigm, centring education on the student, on the skills that need to be developed and on the processes of acquisition and construction of this knowledge (Michavila and Esteve 2011).

To efficiently achieve these objectives the teaching staff must define and put forward their mission and design and develop their own educational project. A project should take into account three specific things (Esteve Mon and Gisbert Cervera 2011):

- That the student is the centre of the learning process.
- That an active teaching methodology favours the formation of more versatile and employable people and professionals.
- That one learns in a permanent way and that it is necessary to follow this process also in a permanent way. To this end continuous evaluation will be key to be able to show that the proposed learning objectives have been completed.

Cooperative learning makes sense when learning is conceived as something active, constructed by the student with other students and teaching staff. The students' autonomy is taken as read, and is necessary for them to be able to assume personal responsibility and to be able to take decisions for themselves in the development of the task.

11.2 Active Methodologies

Students need to adapt themselves to a learning system based on competences, whose objective does not only consist of a progressive accumulation of general and specific knowledge, but also the acquisition of capacities and/or abilities for the achievement of academic results. In this way active methodologies need to promote, acquire and/or consolidate the transversal skills necessary for the integral preparation of the student, including teamwork, oral and written communication, capacity for analysis and summary, the use of new methodologies for information research, amongst others.

There exists a great variety of activities that promote active learning, helping the student to "learn to learn" through skills development. Autonomy in learning can be understood as the "ability to make decisions that allow the regulation of one's own learning, aiming towards a predetermined end, within the protection of certain specific conditions which form the context of the learning" (Monereo 2001). To achieve more autonomous students means making them aware of the decisions they take, of the knowledge available, of the difficulties in learning and of the way of overcoming these difficulties.

To this end, as teachers we must orient the methodologies used towards the goal of our students as autonomous, strategic, reflective, cooperative and responsible learners. Active learning requires that different methodologies that strengthen the participation and independent work of the students are combined. The professor ceases to be the principal source of knowledge and consultation, although they will of course accompany and guide the student throughout the learning process (Álvarez Pérez and González Afonso 2005). With this in mind, it is advisable to use a group of methods that promote the involvement of the student in tasks such as: teamwork, analysis, summary and evaluation, development of strategies in which the student, as well as taking part, reflects upon the action being developed (Hargreaves and Fink 2006).

Teamwork involves a small number of people with complementary knowledge and skills bringing together their abilities to complete certain objectives and to undertake activities aimed at the achievement of these objectives (Ander-Egg and Aguilar 2001). It is also important to provide basic information about the teamwork before starting to use this technique (Viles et al. 2012).

Given the type of course to be offered, the student profile has to be taken into account, in this case they are workers from a particular company, and as Mantilla and García (2010) say, these days manual workers have become intellectual workers, they have information about how the processes should be run, they observe tendencies, identify irregularities and take decisions. All this was important when laying out the course. Some of the tools used in the course are briefly outlined below.

11.2.1 Aronson Puzzle

Within the array of cooperative work tools is the one known as Jigsaw or Puzzle, by Aronson and Osherow (1980). Materials must be prepared by the professor beforehand, given that the theme to be worked by the students needs to be distributed in various parts as if they were pieces of a puzzle (Mayorga and Madrid Vivar 2012).

1. Distribution. After dividing the students into small and homogenous groups the professor hands out the material. This is divided into parts, relatively independent, numbering the same as the number of group members. In our work we formed groups of five components.
2. Individual study. Each member of the group studies the academic content they have been given and becomes an expert in it.
3. Meeting of experts. The members belonging to different groups that have studied the same content meet in an "experts' group" to clear up any doubts and to go into detail on the topic.
4. Individual preparation. Each member of the group prepares a strategy to explain their section to the other members of the group.
5. Explanations in the base group. Each student returns to their original group and, in order, explains their part to the other members.

The evaluation of the knowledge acquired can be done in group or individual form. The evaluation system can be undertaken equally through a coevaluation or heteroevaluation.

11.2.2 The Case Method

GIMA (2004) defines the case as "a vehicle or tool through which a real problem is brought to the classroom so that students and professors conscientiously examine the situation presented and then develop, through the discussion generated, knowledge and abilities, attitudes and values in agreement with the objectives specific to the session and general to the course".

The case method is a technique that implements active learning strategies, based on the description of a situation or context, in which a problem or group of questions is considered. This promotes the ability to develop reasoned answers to circumstances and is used to motivate critical and strategic thinking as much as to develop abilities in communication and presentation of answers to the cases. The active participation of the student is required in real and hypothetical situations that reflect experiences typically found in the area of study. With this the student puts into practice skills which can be transferred into the workplace.

Utilizing this methodology it is possible, with any theme, to have a graphical vision of the dynamic and of the component relationships.

The principle advantage of this method is that it is a motivational methodology that develops abilities of analysis and synthesis, which means that the content is more significant for the students. For it to work it is imperative that the case has been correctly put together and presented and that the students' tasks are clearly defined. It is important to reflect upon the learning goals achieved with the students.

11.3 Experience

The participants in this educational innovation were all the students from the company enrolled on the course. In total 50 students were split into two groups of 25 (one in the morning and another in the afternoon). Within each group of 25 were performed five working groups of five students each. Courses with similar themes had been given previously at the same company. On previous occasions traditional teaching methods were used. This has been the first occasion in this company when active methodologies were used in our courses. During and after the realization of the course results were observed, which will be commented upon in the conclusion.

11.3.1 Proposed Objectives

The principal objectives of the teaching innovation undertaken were:

1. Establish of what the group relationships, the dynamics and techniques of the group consisted of.

2. To know the level of student satisfaction with respect to active methodologies used.
3. That the students know and utilize different generic competences, especially that of group work.

11.3.2 Evaluation Instruments

Different questionnaires were adapted about:

1. The rating of the active methodologies used (Aronson's Puzzle and Case Study) by means firstly of a group presentation and secondly a case resolution. Both were group evaluations.
2. The individually acquired competences and abilities during the course. This was by means of an objective test and open questions.

11.3.3 Group Composition

The number of group components for each activity was five people. This number could appear to be high for certain types of task and small for others, but we would prefer to maintain the groups for this study.

11.3.4 Teaching Methodologies Used

The principal methodologies used for this work have been: group dynamics, collaborative learning and Aronson's Puzzle, study of engineering-related cases and participative presentation method. The utilization of some of these is explained in point 2 of this chapter. All the students took part in all of them.

These methodologies were later evaluated by means of individual evaluation (a small objective test and another of open questions) and group evaluation (a paper combining the answers brought up during the case studies as well as a group oral presentation in class).

11.4 Results

The ratings can be divided as can be seen below (Fig. 11.1).

In general, this teaching methodology (fairly new to the students) was well received by the students.

The group of very positive ratings stands out because the students use adjectives such as "pleasant", "appropriate", "participative", "dynamic", "enjoyable" or

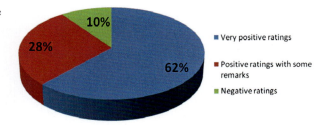

Fig. 11.1 Percentages of the ratings. *Source*: own production

"enriching". It was commented that amongst the advantages of this teaching method were the fact that it allows the contrasting of various people's opinions, moving away from the master lecture where the teacher's opinions prevail, and the class proved less monotonous; something which allows more relaxed learning and maintains attention levels.

With respect to the positive ratings with comments, the fact that some students mention having learning problems with these new methods in spite of having given a generally good rating stands out. Also some students prefer individual teaching although they liked the method. It was commented that not all students participated in the same way in the group work.

There were only five negative ratings which were not very well justified, and we gained ideas for improvement more from other more positive ratings than from these. Some students thought that this form of learning would penalize them in terms of results, which proved totally false once it was observed that the results obtained in this course, when compared with one along similar lines from the previous year, had improved. The average for the course increased by 1.5 points (out of 10).

11.5 Conclusions and Proposals for Future Actuations

The main conclusion that can be extracted from this work is the favourable evaluation given to the methodologies by the students. These methodologies lead to the active participation of the students in a system of continuous evaluation in which the grading of the student does not only depend upon the final exam. The work presented here confirms that this methodology motivates the student to continuously follow the course. The actual students also positively assess these techniques because, despite the fact that they recognise that they require more dedication, they consider that the techniques oblige them to study the material on a daily basis, and consequently gain a better understanding of the material and better academic results. Although the marks have not been published yet, they were better than previous courses with different methodologies. As was mentioned in the previous section the average rose by 1.5 points out of 10.

The professors are satisfied with the excellent reception given to the applied methodology by the students, but it is important to point out that the application of this teaching methodology means a high level of effort and volume of work for the professor, which is not sufficiently recognised or valued.

This paper has also tried to observe the influence that active methodologies can have for use in learning in industrial environments, given that they are not only university teaching methods. It is worth indicating that in general those students whose companies oblige them to attend classes often become bored, abandon the course or fail the final exam, but this was not this case here. Which is to say that we achieved more motivated students that finished the course and benefitted from it.

As non-tangible benefits of the course, an improvement in the group work processes was observed, as well as greater involvement and motivation of the workers attending the course, raised awareness of the actions and importance as well as a greater sense of security when taking decisions and non-repetitive actions. The benefit commented upon here was observed afterwards, and it was the management of the said groups that pointed out this improvement.

The results obtained encourage the continued promotion of experiments that favour group work, for the positive effects that they can have on determined factors that occur as much in learning as in professional development.

References

Álvarez Pérez P, González Afonso M (2005) La Tutoría Académica en la Enseñanza Superior: una Estrategia Docente ante el Nuevo Reto de la Convergencia Europea. Rev Electrón Interuniversitaria Formación Profesorado 8(4):1–4

Ander-Egg E, Aguilar MJ (2001) El Trabajo en Equipo. Editorial Progreso S.A, México

Aronson E, Osherow N (1980) Cooperation, prosocial behaviour and academic performance. Appl Soc Psychol Ann 1:163–196. Editorial L. Bickman

De Miguel Díaz M (Dir) (2006) Metodologías de Enseñanza y Aprendizaje para el Desarrollo de Competencias. Orientaciones para el Profesorado Universitario ante el Espacio Europeo de Educación Superior. Alianza Editorial

Esteve Mon FM, Gisbert Cervera M (2011) El Nuevo Paradigma de Aprendizaje y las Nuevas Tecnologías. Rev Docencia Universitaria 9(3):55–73

GIMA (2004) El método del Caso. Ficha Descriptiva de Necesidades. Universidad Politécnica de Valencia. Grupo de Metodologías Activas. http://www.upv.es/nume/descargas/fichamdc.pdf

Hargreaves A, Fink D (2006) Estrategias de Cambio y Mejora en Educación Caracterizadas por su Relevancia, difusión y Continuidad en el Tiempo. Rev Educ 339:43–58. http://www.revistaeducacion.mec.es/re339/re339_04.pdf

Mantilla M, García D (2010) Trabajo en Equipos Autodirigidos: Competencias Personales y Conductas Necesarias para su Éxito. Rev Venez Gerencia 15(49):51–71. Universidad de Zulia. Venezuela

Mayorga MJ, Madrid Vivar D (2012) La Técnica del Puzzle como Estrategia de Aprendizaje Cooperativo para la Mejora del Rendimiento Académico. Publicaciones, vol 42. http://hdl.handle.net/10481/24750

MEC (2006) Directrices para la Elaboración de Títulos Universitarios de Grado y Máster (Propuesta, de 21 de diciembre, de la Secretaría de Estado de Universidades e Investigación). MEC, Madrid

Michavila F, Esteve F (2011) La Llegada a la Universidad: ¿Oportunidad o Amenaza? CEE Participación Educ 17:69–85

Monereo C (2001) Ser Estratégico y Autónomo Aprendiendo. Unidades didácticas de enseñanza estratégica. Editorial GRAÓ, de IRIF, S.L. Barcelona

Viles E, Jaca C, Campos J, Serrano N, Santos J (2012) Evaluación de la Competencia de Trabajo en Equipo en los Grados de Ingeniería. Dirección Organización 46:67–75

Villardón L, Yániz C (2003) Estilos de Aprendizaje y Aprendizaje Cooperativo. Actas del Congreso Internacional Humanismo para el siglo XXI. Publicado en CD. Bilbao

Chapter 12
Co-creation Innovation Model for Masters Programs in the Universities

Gabriela Ribes-Giner, Agustin Peralt Rillo, and Ismael Moya Clemente

Abstract The purpose of this study is to offer a model that facilitates innovation for postgraduate institutions as they develop masters under the concept of co-creation innovation and its necessary proactive market orientation. First, we provide a comprehensive literature review related to "universities" and "innovation for higher education institutions" and the "co-creation innovation" paradigm. Second, we use the Delphi technique to further validate the analysis of literature and develop a model that facilitates innovation for postgraduate institutions for their postgraduate programs, under the concept of co-creation which integrates the different stakeholders which participate in this process, university staff and teachers, adult students, and employers. Finally, we highlight that such a model has the ability to provide different ways to facilitate the innovation process in a coherent way and help universities to find a differentiation strategy and to be much more adapted to the needs of companies and adult students. Through a comprehensive literature review of the concepts of proactive market orientation for educational innovation and co-creation innovation, we have created a framework for improving the innovation among those institutions for this particular segment of postgraduate students. This tool has the potential to facilitate the interaction among customers, companies, universities, and all stakeholders under the co-creating innovation paradigm.

G. Ribes-Giner (✉) • A.P. Rillo
Departamento de Organización de Empresas, Universidad Politécnica de Valencia, Camino de Vera, s/n 46022, Valencia, Spain
e-mail: gabrigi@omp.upv.es

I.M. Clemente
Rectorado, Universidad Politécnica de Valencia, Camino de Vera, s/n 46022, Valencia, Spain
e-mail: imoya@esp.upv.es

12.1 Literature Review

12.1.1 The Linkage Between Universities, Market Orientation, and Innovation

In the global context postgraduate education has become an industry in itself like, for example, the United States, where higher education is estimated to employ 3.4 million people, and represent 3 % of the entire country's service sector OECD (2011). Postgraduate education can be considered as a service where the universities, employers, and the adult students have an important role because they participate in the process (Kotler and Fox 1995). Pusina et al. (2008) also state that it can be viewed as a purchase of service, with universities and faculties as service sellers and adult students as customers. Venkatesh (2001) recommended that programs of postgraduate should be marketed on the basis of service marketing. When considering the particular consideration of the educational programs as a service, Toivonen and Tuominen (2009) present the following complete definition for a service innovation: "service innovation is a new service or such a renewal of an existing service which is put into practice and which provides benefits to the organization that has developed it; the benefit usually derives from the added value that the renewal provides to the customers."

On the one hand, when focusing on the higher education market and its customers, Kotler and Fox (1995) proposed that in the educational sector the only consideration of the product innovation approach is that the new products have to be created to satisfy two different needs, the students' and employers' ones. In addition, Enache (2011) mentioned that these new programs have to take into consideration not only the students' needs but also the labor market needs. It is highly accepted that the sector has multi-clients, as students, employers, and society are seen to be the main beneficiaries of postgraduate services (Maringe 2006). While students are the primary consumers, employers can be seen as secondary or indirect consumers of postgraduate services (Nocolescu et al. 2009). So as Taylor and Reed (1995) noted, marketing of postgraduate does not mean taking a totally student-centric perspective, but rather that the needs of various stakeholders need to be balanced.

On the other hand, when considering the role of the educational institutions, Chapleo (2004) stated that there is a lack of real differentiation in the educational sector in general. He considers that in spite of the similarity of products offered, key factors could be pursued by universities to occupy positions of distinctiveness. In this increasing competitive situation, it is obviously the need for strategies that lead the sector. Moreover, Nocolescu et al. (2009) posed that the marketing field is still to be developed and adapted for the postgraduate sector, and that in addition to the promotion and communication, there are many other actions for satisfying the student which have to be considered. Also, Temple and Shattock (2007) noted that most universities are actually doing very much like most other universities. Enache (2011) suggested that a framework able to provide relevant information and suitable instruments will improve the market presence of any postgraduate institution. To the same effect, Maringe and Gibbs (2009) found that one of the new lessons universities are learning from business and the commercial world today is how to develop a customer perspective. Voorhess (2005) indicated that it is necessary to use different techniques to assess the market potential of new programs. Kotler and Keller (2009) also stated that formulating a postgraduate institutional marketing strategy includes among others decision about the institution's current programs and future new programs (product innovation) as long as designing the rest of the marketing mix (other types of innovation).

Considering the need for a market orientation in the educational market in order to achieve a successful innovation policy, Liu and Dubinsky (2000) proposed a strategic path for universities transiting from a paternalistic government funding to a market-oriented setting.

The present study recognizes the relevance of utilizing market orientation and differentiation as a way of innovation in higher education. The authors propose that this knowledge enables university administrators to gain a better understanding of graduate students so that they can improve their marketing techniques to more effectively recruit and retain goal-oriented students who can successfully achieve their degrees.

12.1.2 Co-creation Innovation

In the early 1990s, Song and Adams (1993) already suggested that customer participation should not be examined under the aspect of cost minimization. Instead it could be seen as an opportunity to differentiate. Since then, and related to these theories of market orientation, which have been reviewed previously, many scholars have been working on the concept of co-creation as a higher consumer-focused strategy. Prahalad and Ramaswamy (2004) introduced the co-creation concept as a unique way to creating value for customers. They insisted that companies can no longer act autonomously, designing products and developing production processes with little or no interference from consumers. Consumers want to interact with firms and thereby co-create value. Vargo and Lusch (2004) defined this co-creation concept as the way companies deal with their customers through customer participation in the joint creation of service value. According to the latest developments in service research, value co-creation is a central concept generally applicable to the service (Díaz-Méndez and Gummesson 2012). In this proactive market orientation, the customer takes part as a collaborative partner, jointly co-creating value with the company. According to Kristenson et al. (2002), involving users as co-creators during new product development (product innovation) produces ideas that are more creative, more highly valued by customers, and more easily implemented. Several studies have shown that user involvement leads to innovative ideas. In particular, user involvement is reported to be useful for capturing the latent needs of consumers that are so important to successful new product development (Kristenson et al. 2002). This new co-creation framework implies that all the points of consumer–company interaction are critical for creating value (Prahalad and Ramaswamy 2003). The same authors state that for now every customer wants to be part or have influence in the business system, and wants to interact with the company and co-create value together. From a managerial perspective, this suggests that it is beneficial when working with incremental innovation to spend time with customers, or become immersed in the customer's context as much as possible (Witell et al. 2011). Essentially, customer co-creation concerns different ways of communicating and interacting with customers and their context during the value co-creation process (Gustafsson et al. 2012). Baldwin and Von Hippel (2010) argued that in many industries, new product and service ideas come from lead users, that is, a customer who utilizes the product or service in extreme conditions and effectively helps the company co-create new offerings as a result. Hasche (2006) concluded that the focus has shifted from the activities performed by the firm to activities co-created in a relationship with other partners and stakeholders.

In sum, the existing literature clearly emphasizes that customer participation in value co-creation activities should impact their innovation outcomes, such as innovation cost, time to market, new product, and development capacity (Bowonder et al. 2010; Kristensson et al. 2008; Nambisan and Baron 2009; Prahalad and Krishnan 2008; Ramaswamy and Gouillart 2010). For universities, it would be beneficial to spend time with customers or, in other words, become immersed in the customer's context as much as possible as the only way a company can form an opinion about the customer's real needs (Witell et al. 2011).

Finally, the concept of co-creation is of vital importance for our educational market. It is critical that we utilize its potential in the educational services for postgraduate programs where the opinion of adult students, faculty, staff, and employers is key for the process of co-creating of educational programs that are meaningful, efficient, and innovative. As the Fraunhofer Institute research studies found, universities are not still benefiting from the whole potential of co-creation and are not involving their students in the daily business to contribute to improve (Gallouj and Djellall 2011).

12.2 Methodology

The purpose of this study was to develop and validate a framework of co-creation innovation in the postgraduate market. We utilized a two-round Delphi Survey. This method has proven to be an effective and valid tool in business research for identifying, prioritizing, and validating issues for managerial decision making by achieving consensus among panelists (Alsmadi and Khan 2010). Holsapple and Joshi (2000) used a Delphi approach to develop the final framework from an initial one. In phase one of the Delphi technique, a packet of information was emailed to each of the reviewers. The reviewers were asked to respond within 1 week to questions related to the relation between adult student, employer, and university members considering the relation proposed by Peralt-Rillo and Riber-Giner (2013); information about

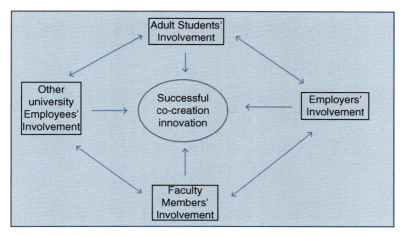

Adapted from Ribes & Peralt (2012)

Fig. 12.1 Stakeholders involved in co-creation innovation for masters programs

the adult student or the employer which could be useful in order to have further researches; different types of innovation in higher education which should be considered in this co-creation.

In this first round, the panel members were asked to judge the relations between adult student, employers, and university members as the different participants for the co-creation paradigm and also, to propose influence factors or new inputs in order to include in the proposed model. Their written responses were reviewed and grouped together based on the questions asked, the area of the model addressed, and miscellaneous feedback. These responses were then summarized by category: (1) changes to be introduced in the relation between the stakeholders; (2) key information to be researched and to be introduced in the model; (3) other types of innovation to be considered.

The panel of experts recommended the following revisions in the proposed model.

It should provide a more detailed relation between the stakeholders in which all the possible relations are considered. The changes are presented in Fig 12.1.

There should be additional researches which should be considered taking into account that the employer is the one which starts the process and even takes the final decision for its employee.

It should consider also types of innovation related to the relation and the participation of the employer.

The main purpose of the second round was to confirm the modified framework based on the first-round feedback. In the second round, after having introduced the modifications from the first round, they were asked to confirm the overall modified framework. Thus, only a single question was posed. The question asked: "Can you agree with this model?" Each one responded "yes" and Round Two was complete; the Delphi study ended. No further changes were made to model presented in Fig. 12.2.

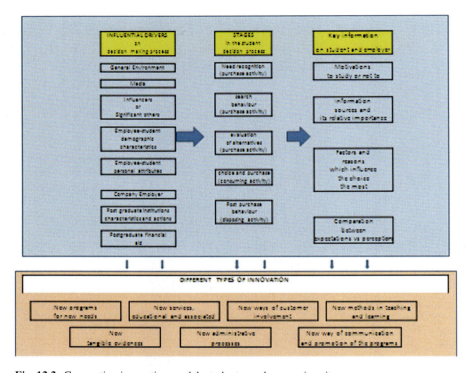

Fig. 12.2 Co-creation innovation model: student–employer–university

12.3 Results

On the one hand, as commented, Fig. 12.1 deals with the relations between adult students, employers, and university members as the different participants for the co-creation paradigm considering the opinions of our panel experts and the changes they proposed. The result is a more detailed relation between all the stakeholders with all the different relations which are presented in it. The different influences among them are what could be considered interrelations with multiple affections. It is important to highlight the importance of considering all these different relations as vital to be able to get profit from an innovation process like this.

On the other hand, our model (Fig. 12.2) starts with the different drivers which influence the different phases of the decision making process for this adult student. In these influential drivers, all the different actors which appeared in Fig. 12.1 are considered for their influence on the adult student. Consequently, this model is the first step in order to integrate both the adult student and the employer in this need for innovation in the educational market as a way of differentiating. The decision making process will be the origin of the key information which can be obtained. This information will be vital in order to understand this adult student behavior which is considered of high implication. As Kotler and Keller (2009) stated this consumer behavior is a key source of knowledge, which can help to innovate in a successful way as a source of a differentiation strategy. According to this statement, our model finally highlights the different types of innovation which can be considered when deciding to start a co-creation innovation process. In this final scheme developed, we have tried to reflect all the possibilities which may exist to connect our new adult decision model and its possibilities of future studies. This may help to create different types of innovation, all under the participation of the main stakeholders: adult students, employers, and faculty and university staff. In our model, the point of departure is, as mentioned, the decision making process and the drivers, which influence each of its phases or stages. These stages will help us to consider the key information we should take into account in order to get knowledge for the future innovation policy.

Thus, when considering a product innovation in the educational sector, working under this co-creation framework will help to increase the probability of great successful innovations which satisfy everybody's needs, and even more when considering the postgraduate programs where some of the adult students' companies are involved.

As mentioned before, and as we can see in our Fig. 12.1, our co-creation approach for innovation considers all the stakeholders involved: adult students, employers or companies and personnel from postgraduate institutions, and faculty and staff working together under this innovation paradigm. This study resulted in a validated model that should be useable by the administrators of universities in order to innovate under the co-creation paradigm.

12.4 Conclusions

The main objective of this study was to propose a framework that facilitated innovation for postgraduate programs under the concept of co-creation (university, adult student, and employers), and its necessary proactive market orientation. The proposed model offers, as an output, different types of future innovations, which the postgraduate institutions should consider and indeed, under the co-creation paradigm. We firmly believe that it offers a wide range of possibilities for innovation as a way of differentiation in this complex educational market, in a way where the possibility of success is higher from our point of view. This competitive advantage will be related to improved productivity and effectiveness with a better fit with customer needs, for example, of co-created products.

The first important key point of our model is that universities involve both adult students and employers in a deep consideration of a proactive market orientation. This co-creation approach is one step forward from the market research techniques. Therefore, with this proactive market orientation, the adult student and employers take a part as collaborative partners co-creating value with the company for both the university and themselves. The relation between these three groups has multiple points of interaction, in which the knowledge about individuals' needs and expectations is generated in order to get a better understanding to satisfy all of these stakeholders.

Finally, we suggest that one of the highest priorities for future research must be focused on this co-creation concept but from the company's point of view, with the collaboration between companies, in our case the postgraduate institutions. In co-creation, from the company's point of view, it will be necessary to review the desire and possibility for the postgraduate institutions to co-create value with other institutions because they might not have enough skills, resources, and competence to develop it by themselves. Future research is needed to validate this model in other countries. Comparative studies can provide a better understanding of the variables affecting the successful application of this model.

References

Alsmadi M, Khan Z (2010) Lean sigma: the new wave of business excellence, literature review and a framework, engineering systems management and its applications (ICESMA), 2010 Second International Conference on 2010, IEEE, pp 1–8

Baldwin C, Von Hippel E (2010) Modeling a paradigm shift: from producer innovation to user and open collaborative innovation. Harvard Business School Finance Working Paper, (10–038), 4764–09

Bowonder B, Dambal A, Kumar S, Shirodkar A (2010) Innovation strategies for creating competitive advantage. Res Technol Manage 53(3):19–32

Chapleo C (2004) Interpretation and implementation of reputation/brand management by UK university leaders. Int J Educ Advance 5(1):7–23

Díaz-Méndez M, Gummesson E (2012) Value co-creation and university teaching quality: consequences for the European Higher Education Area (EHEA). J Serv Manage 23(4):571–592

Enache I (2011) Marketing higher education using the 7 Ps framework. Bull Transilvania Univ Braşov 4(1):23

Gallouj F, Djellall F (2011) The handbook of innovation and services: a multi-disciplinary perspective. Edward Elgar, Northampton

Gustafsson A, Kristensson P, Witell L (2012) Customer co-creation in service innovation: a matter of communication? J Serv Manage 23(3):311–327

Hasche N (2006) Developing collaborative customer-supplier relationships through value co-creation

Holsapple C, Joshi K (2000) An investigation of factors that influence the management of knowledge in organizations. J Strat Inform Syst 9(2):235–261

Kotler P, Fox KF (1995) Strategic Marketing for educational institutions. Prentice Hall

Kotler P, Keller K (2009) Marketing Management: International Edition. Pearson Education

Kristenson P, Magnusson PR, Matthing J (2002) Users as a hidden resource for creativity: findings from an experimental study on user involvement. Creativity Innov Manage 11(1):55–61

Kristensson P, Matthing J, Johansson N (2008) Key strategies for the successful involvement of customers in the co-creation of new technology-based services. Int J Serv Ind Managem 19(4):474–491

Liu SS, Dubinsky AJ (2000) Institutional entrepreneurship—a panacea for universities-in-transition? Eur J Market 34(11/12):1315–1337

Maringe F (2006) University and course choice: implications for positioning, recruitment and marketing. Int J Educ Manage 20(6):466–479

Maringe F, Gibbs P (2009) Marketing higher education: theory and practice. Open University Press, Buckingham

Nambisan S, Baron RA (2009) Virtual customer environments: testing a model of voluntary participation in value co-creation activities. J Prod Innov Manage 26(4):388–406

Nocolescu L, Pricopie R, Popescu A (2009) Country differences in the internationalization of higher education–how can countries lagging behind diminish the gap. Rev Int Comp Manage 10(5)

OECD (2011) Education at a glance. OECD

Peralt-Rillo A, Riber-Giner G (2013) A proactive market orientation for the postgraduate programs. Dirección y Organización 50:37–47

Prahalad C, Krishnan MMS (2008) The new age of innovation. McGraw-Hill Professional, New York

Prahalad CK, Ramaswamy V (2003) The new frontier of experience innovation. MIT Sloan Manage Rev 44(4):12–18

Prahalad CK, Ramaswamy V (2004) Co-creating unique value with customers. Strat Leadership 32(3):4–9

Pusina A, Basic H, Pestek A (2008) Active learning methods in the context of higher education reform. Zbornik radova Ekonomskog fakulteta u Sarajevu 28:132

Ramaswamy V, Gouillart F (2010) Building the co-creative enterprise. Harv Bus Rev 88(10):100–109

Song JH, Adams CR (1993) Differentiation through customer involvement in production or delivery. J Cons Market 10(2):4–12

Taylor RE, Reed RR (1995) Situational marketing: application for higher education institutions. J Market Higher Educ 6(1):23–36

Temple P, Shattock M (2007) What does "branding mean in Higher Education?". EAIR

Toivonen M, Tuominen T (2009) Emergence of innovations in services. Serv Ind J 29(7):887–902

Vargo SL, Lusch RF (2004) Evolving to a new dominant logic for marketing. J Market 68:1–17

Venkatesh U (2001) The importance of managing points-of-marketing in marketing higher education programs–some conclusions. J Serv Res 1(1):125–140

Voorhess RA (2005) Institutional research and new program development. New Dir Inst Res 2005(128):29–39

Witell L, Kristensson P, Gustafsson A, Lofgren M (2011) Idea generation: customer co-creation versus traditional market research techniques. J Serv Manage 22(2):140–150

Chapter 13
Wearable Computers and Big Data: Interaction Paradigms for Knowledge Building in Higher Education

Roberto Llorente and Maria Morant

Abstract Recent advances in computing and telecommunication technology have made powerful wearable computers available. They are always connected to a wireless infrastructure with batteries and last an entire day, all for reasonable price. Examples of such computers currently available on the market are Google Glass wearable intelligent glasses and the Sony Smartwatch wearable wristwatch. For the first time, interconnected devices worn by the professor that communicate with a large computing infrastructure permit massive data extraction (known as "big data" resources), which can be data-mined to monitor the knowledge-building process, thus maximizing efficiency in higher education environments.

13.1 Introduction

The continuous increase in computing capabilities of digital personal devices (e.g., cell phones and tablets) has opened up the possibility of developing target-specific software applications for educational purposes. Over the past few years, several learning-targeted software applications have emerged. Their purpose is to provide personalized learning experiences through mobile devices (Looi et al. 2009). The integration of mobile technologies into the learning process is an important part of the development of technical-enabled advanced forms of education (Yordanova 2007).

R. Llorente (✉)
Departamento de Comunicaciones, Universitat Politècnica de València,
Camino de Vera, s/n 46022, Valencia, Spain
e-mail: rllorent@dcom.upv.es

M. Morant
Centro de Tecnología Nanofónica, Universitat Politècnica de València,
Camino de Vera, s/n 46022, Valencia, Spain
e-mail: mmorant@ntc.upv.es

M. Peris-Ortiz et al. (eds.), *Innovation and Teaching Technologies: New Directions in Research, Practice and Policy*, DOI 10.1007/978-3-319-04825-3_13,
© Springer International Publishing Switzerland 2014

Nowadays, pedagogical approaches present a combination of conventional lecturing paradigms and ICT (information and communications technology) in an enhanced lecturing experience. The pervasive presence of mobile technology leads to the introduction of the mobile-learning (m-learning) based on ubiquitous wireless connectivity. In this scenario, wearable computers, such as wearable intelligent glasses, smartwatches combined with high-tech smartphones, or tablets, may be pointed out as the next step in educational technology in the classroom.

In this chapter, we propose a novel paradigm in technology-assisted education: the use of wearable computers connected to a wireless infrastructure in order to gather thoughtful data, monitoring the lecturing process in order to be processed, and targeting to maximize performance of the knowledge-building process.

13.2 Wearable Computers Today

Different formats of wearable computers, from smartwatches to intelligent glasses, are already available on the market through major technology companies. Different factors that should be taken into account in adopting wearable computers are as follows:

- First, the wearable computer has to provide a clear advantage at work and in day-to-day tasks. Two key aspects are relevant here: underlying technical capabilities and the so-called application ecosystem. Technical capabilities of wearable computers are expected to continue improving as far as better sensory capabilities and computing capacity are concerned, as has already occurred with cell phone technology (Lawler 2013). The software application environment is usually based on standard platforms, such as Android. This indicates that a large number of applications are readily available.
- Second, the wearable computer must be easy to wear. Of course, this should be achieved through proper ergonomic design. This way, it would be easy to make the habit of wearing the device. A long-term strategy depicted by some manufacturers is embedding wearable computers into clothing (McClusky 2009). However, this approach requires a sharp decline in hardware price.

After widespread adoption, educators must take advantage of the pervasive presence of these computers in the classroom. In using wearable computers, people will be able to learn wherever they choose, without needing to be tied down to a particular location, by using broadcast media and online access (Sharples 2000). Wearable computer technology combined with pervasive online connectivity makes the paradigm of personal highly portable communication devices a reality. Following this early paradigm, it is clear that wearable devices in the educational environment must permit complete freedom of movement around the classroom. The light weight of these devices should make them non-obtrusive within the learning space (Looi et al. 2009), not interfering in the classic lecturing process for which most lecturers are trained. It is clear then that wearable technology is the right path in moving toward an enhanced lecturing process, strongly based on the traditional lecturing process, i.e., with minimum disruption in the classroom that we already know (Vallurupalli et al. 2013).

13.2.1 Wearable Computer Technology

Wearable computers are devices which provide information to the user, all while interacting with the environment. The first wearable computer was made in the 1960s by mathematicians Edward O. Thorp and Claude Shannon, comprising a computerized timer concealed in a cigarette pack, or in a shoe, that was used to predict the roulette (Thorp 1998). Since 1980, technology has reduced the size and weight of personal computers, thereby making "wearing it" a possibility. Over the past few years, the advances in high-performance sensors and microprocessors—requiring less space and power—applied to wearable devices allowed the automatic capture of data while interacting with the environment (Martin and Siewiorek 1994). Wearable technology is applied to manufacturing processes, self-guided navigation, and medicine (Martin and Siewiorek 1994). However, some obstacles in bringing wearable technology into education still exist.

Wearable technology has been recently used within a medical educational environment. For example, in 2013, Google Glass was used to explore different scenarios in cardiovascular practice, enabling fellows to improve their learning (Vallurupalli et al. 2013). In the feasibility study carried out at the University of Arkansas for Medical Sciences, streaming live video, recorded through the glasses, was transmitted via Wi-Fi or Bluetooth. This stream could be received by other fellows who were using a smartphone, tablet, or personal computer. The main advantage of using a wearable hands-free device in a medical application is that aid can be instantly sought from experts anywhere in the world without infringing on sterile precautions (Vallurupalli et al. 2013).

In the academic environment, hands-free use devices are also preferred (Starner 2002), so as to be able to interact within the classroom without needing to hold a device. Head-mounted displays can be used in the educational field to show augmented-reality content, such as the Past Viewer system that overlays past and present scenes on a see-through display (Nakasugi and Yamauchi 2002). Wearable computing can also be useful for in-field learning. In 2006, the National Institute of Multimedia Education developed a learning support system to provide appropriate location-awareness information in the field (Osawa and Asai 2006).

In this chapter, we present the possibilities of using wearable technology to acquire and process data to efficiently gain knowledge in higher education.

13.2.2 Market-Available Devices

Technical advances in battery efficiency, augmented-reality displays, and semiconductor integrated circuit manufacturing have expanded the market for wearable devices as of the year 2013. Relevant wearable technology categories available on the market are shown in Fig. 13.1. Firstly, we can find smartwatches, which are computerized wristwatches with enhanced functionalities beyond timekeeping. It appears that the NL C01 Pulsar was the first watch capable of storing 24 digits with calculation functionality in 1982. Since then, smartwatches have evolved into wearable computers running mobile apps, including other features such as a camera, cell

Fig. 13.1 Wearable device categories and notable devices available on the market as of 2013

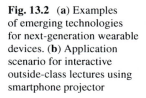
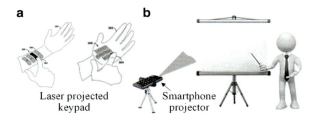

Fig. 13.2 (a) Examples of emerging technologies for next-generation wearable devices. (b) Application scenario for interactive outside-class lectures using smartphone projector

phone, GPS navigation, and accelerometer. In January 2013, Pebble smartwatch was mass produced. In September 2013, the new watches Samsung Galaxy Gear and Sony SmartWatch 2 were launched.

Another type of wearable computer devices are based on glasses. Google Glass is an optical head-mounted display (OHMD) that shows information in a smartphone-like hands-free format, enabling interaction with the Internet via voice commands. Although Google Glass is currently in a developmental stage, it is expected to be available to the general public in 2014. Other companies are also developing enhanced-reality glasses. For instance, Samsung has recently patented (as of October 2013) a new design for smartphone-connected sport glasses. There is also the possibility of developing your own intelligent glasses with commercially available components (Furlan 2013).

Wearable devices are also used as body sensors. Several activity-tracking devices are available, such as Nike's Fuelband® or Jawbone's Up® wristbands. Rest Devices' Mimo is the first wearable device oriented toward newborn babies that is able to detect changes in a baby's temperature, motion, and respiration.

Figure 13.2a shows some examples of next-generation wearable technologies. Recently, Google has applied for a patent to include laser projection in the Google Glass camera. A keypad cast would be projected on a hand and the camera would identify the number or letter pressed. In July 2013, researchers from the University of Tokyo developed a skin-like "indestructible" material that can detect pressure. Also, Nokia's Facet watch with multiple display segments has been patented.

The debate regarding the impact of technology development foresees that the global wearable computer market could be worth $10 billion within the next 3 years (Demianyk 2013). Recent studies (Rackspace 2013) indicate that 82 % of wearable technology users in the USA considered that employing cloud-powered devices enhanced their lives and 33 % of people surveyed said that these devices have helped in their career development (Beighton 2013). Also, more than half of the people polled highlighted that using wearable cloud-powered devices boosted their creativity and personal efficiency (Rackspace 2013).

Legal and security implications of wearable technology must also be considered. For example, Google Glass and smartwatches with built-in cameras will enable the wearer to record everything in real time. This could open a security breach, enabling the transfer of sensitive or classified information to a device outside the network (Demianyk 2013). Wearable device vendors and cloud providers are already working together to enhance the quality of data capture and analysis (Beighton 2013). This will be helpful in order to take better advantage of wearable technologies and related applications in the near future.

13.3 New Classroom Interaction Paradigms

Personalized learning techniques should provide the students with more autonomy to chart their own individual learning paths. As defined in Looi et al. (2009), students are no longer the passive recipients of knowledge. Rather, they are coproducers of the knowledge and they can decide what and how they want to learn. Using mobile technology makes it possible to "move" lectures outside the classroom, bringing them to real application premises such as company offices and subject-related facilities (hospitals, museums, manufacturing premises, etc.).

New smartphones with mobile projectors as shown in Fig. 13.2b allow the professor to project content anywhere. The smartphone can be used to display notes, slides, and audio and video content directly on the ceiling or walls at a close distance—Fig. 13.2b—reaching a size of up to 50″ (as large as a commercial TV). DLP pico projectors are becoming available in a variety of cell phone models. In addition to this, Google Research is working on Open Project, which can make any computer display projectable by using a mere smartphone (Negulescu and Li 2013). Figure 13.3a shows the concept of Google Open Project that transforms the

Fig. 13.3 (**a**) Google Open Project concept transforming coordinates; (**b**) application scenario with projectable computer screen from smartphone; and (**c**) shared drawing pad projected from the smartphone

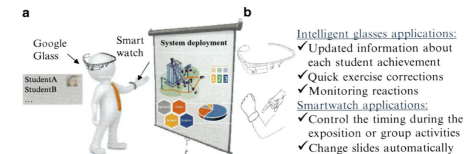

Fig. 13.4 (a) Using wearable devices to improve professor experience and student learning. (b) Wearable devices interaction concepts under development

smartphone camera coordinates to wider display coordinates. This technology can be used for educational purposes, helping the professor to share dynamic diagrams and explanations during laboratory lessons by projecting from a smartphone directly onto the student's laboratory computer, as shown in Fig. 13.3b. Also, this application will enable sharing a drawing pad projected from the smartphone with the classroom, as represented in Fig. 13.3c.

Using Google Glass and a smartwatch in the classroom enables the professor to collect important information regarding student knowledge building and to improve learning efficiency. Figure 13.4a shows the proposed application scenario developed at the Universitat Politècnica de València in November 2013.

The smartwatch can be used to automatically change slides while speaking, enabling freedom of movement around the classroom. The professor can control the timing needed for each concept and the time consumed by each activity.

Google Glass technology can be used to obtain real-time updated information about each student achievement (including academic profile) as shown in Fig. 13.4. Using this information, the professor can provide personalized explanations to achieve more effective knowledge building. Intelligent glasses may also be used to monitor student reactions and to record the questions and answers raised during the lesson. As described in more detail in Sect. 13.4.2, Google Glass could also be used for quick exercise corrections by scanning and processing a given test. Figure 13.4b includes a summary of wearable technology interaction proposed at the Universitat Politècnica de València.

13.4 Big Data and Knowledge Building in Higher Education

The concept of big data indicates relatively large amounts of structured and unstructured data that require advanced processing algorithms in order to be fully analyzed. The kind of data and metrics employed vary depending on the entity type and the application scenario. Big data, in modern applications, implies that raw data is paired with metadata information that increases its value (Soman et al. 2006). Interpretation of big data can bring insight that might not be immediately visible by using traditional methods, finding hidden threads, trends, or patterns that may be invisible to the naked eye. These threads are of utmost importance to monitor and steer the knowledge-building process.

13.4.1 Data Gathering by Wearable Computers

Wearable computers open up seamless gathering of valuable data, useful in monitoring and steering the educational process. Data gathering requires development of software applications supporting the higher education process. This data should be processed through new techniques to enhance the knowledge-building process. The three Vs—meaning volume, velocity, and variety (Laney 2001) referred to the challenge of data management—may be fully applied to the learning process. Massive quantities of data—from student reaction to a specific practice, answers, and time efforts—can be gathered from the wearable computers used by the lecturer.

Big data gathering implies that the data should be structured or completed with metadata. In particular, different data and metadata are proposed to be gathered in support of the learning process:

- Concept data: By capturing slides that are presented in the classroom with wearable computers, software can monitor the exact time and date when a concept is presented, as well as the time spent on each concept. This data can be stored for documentation purposes. In this way, lecturing staff can be sure as to the exact number of concepts to which the student has been introduced over the several years of studies that form higher education curricula.
- Audio metadata: Wearable computers can be used to record the audio from a face-to-face tuition in order to complete the concept data. Audio recording and processing is not only important for documentation purposes—so as to make it available online to other students—but it also enables identification of the student response (e.g., murmurs) while given concepts are presented. Metadata about the presence, level, and duration of murmurs is valuable to the lecturer.
- Video metadata: Wearable computer glasses used by the lecturers enable them to gather video data that can be in-device processed in order to evaluate the degree of stress experienced by the student (heart-rate monitor) in the classroom. This information can be combined with concept data in order to clearly pinpoint the concepts that are most difficult for the student.
- Examination metadata: The development of a real-time correction of "live" tests enables automatic linking of the concepts presented in the classroom to the degree of knowledge building developed by the students. This requires a back-office infrastructure for presenting tests, linking the evaluation to the concepts presented. In-device processing can also be used to quickly gather correction data from tests or problems carried out in writing by students.

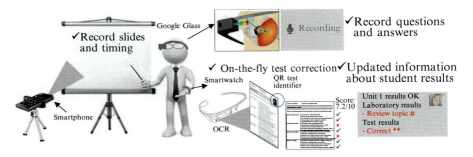

Fig. 13.5 Example of data processing with wearable technology being developed at Universitat Politècnica de València

13.4.2 Wearable Computer Software Applications in Lecturing

Several applications whose purpose is to maximize performance of the lecturing process in higher education by using wearable computers are being developed at the Universitat Politècnica de València. Some examples are as follows:

A. *Presentation slide control and student response monitoring*
   This application presents the slides used in the classroom on an overhead projector. The slides, which move forward via the lecturer smartwatch, are rendered by an Android cell phone. This application can be seen in Fig. 13.5. It records the time spent on each slide, as well as the voices in the classroom. Audio information is processed off-line in order to evaluate the degree of difficulty the students are experiencing with each slide.

   If the lecturers use smart glasses, they can detect the emotions of users upon interacting in an e-learning environment (Lisetti and Nasoz, 2004). Several devices can be used to collect data from users' emotional states: a webcam with an integrated microphone (mostly available currently at higher education facilities), Kinect for face feature extraction, or even a more sophisticated sensor belt with ECG, GSR, and respiratory rate sensors (Santos et al. 2013). Student emotional response during different activities (group activities, problem solving, questionnaires, exams, etc.) can be useful for the professor in evaluating student performance evolution (Chalfoun and Frasson, 2011).

   This application could be further extended, thus eliminating the need of a cell phone, by using wearable glasses as shown in the example depicted in Fig. 13.5. When the professor is wearing Google Glass, he or she can record the questions (and answers) of the students during the lesson. It is also possible to identify a student during the lecture and obtain real-time information, with updated records from his or her previous evaluation. The professor will have exact information regarding the topics each student has understood correctly and which topics need to be reviewed. This is similar to the health application scenario, where the doctor can look at a patient's medical file.

B. *Examination and student metric extraction in the laboratory*
This application takes advantage of the computing infrastructure present in the laboratory. The laboratory time is scheduled to practice the concepts previously introduced in the theoretical lessons; oftentimes, ordinary examinations during laboratory sessions are not accurate and are time-consuming. Using online exercises and questions at the end of the laboratory lesson makes it possible to assess the concepts learned by students in a quick and interactive fashion. A monitoring panel system has been developed at the Universitat Politècnica de València, applying tailored deep data-mining to track the knowledge construction process of engineering students (Llorente and Morant 2011). Data-mining can be applied to evaluate the knowledge building of a given concept. If students observe a question for too long and change the selected response several times, this indicates that the answer is unclear to the students. The results from the monitoring panel are presented to the lecturer in wearable intelligent glasses when looking at a student, so the lecturer can immediately be aware of the difficulties a specific student is experiencing in laboratory assignments. Also, tests solved by hand could by corrected real time with the optical character recognition (OCR), a function of intelligent glasses, as shown in Fig. 13.5. The test can be identified with a quick response (QR) marker and the student score can be automatically calculated.

13.5 Conclusion

This chapter proposes the application of recent advances in wearable computer technology in order to enhance student knowledge building in higher education programs. The availability of reduced and low-cost processors enables the wearable technology market to evolve, with devices such as smartwatches and intelligent glasses. Wearable computers allow one to always be connected to a wireless infrastructure over the course of an entire day, all at a reasonable price. In this chapter, we propose a combination of devices worn by the professor that are connected to a computing infrastructure. This infrastructure enables extraction of big data resources for more efficient knowledge building. The application recently developed at the Universitat Politècnica de València includes the use of a smartwatch to automatically change slides while speaking (permitting free movement around the classroom) and to control and monitor the time consumed by each topic or activity. Intelligent glasses, such as Google Glass, can be used to obtain updated information in real time regarding each student's achievements, including their academic profile. With the combination of wearable technology and big data processing, the professor is able to provide personalized explanations and guidance to the student, thereby achieving more effective knowledge building.

References

Beighton N (2013) The human cloud: wearable technology's impact on society filed in cloud industry insights. Rackspace. http://www.rackspace.com/blog/the-human-cloud-wearable-technologys-impact-on-society/. Accessed 28 Oct 2013

Chalfoun P, Frasson C (2011) Subliminal cues while teaching: HCI technique for enhanced learning. Adv Hum-Comput Interact 2011:1–15

Demianyk S (2013) The impact of wearable tech on office IT security. Real business. http://realbusiness.co.uk/p/24308. Accessed 21 Oct 2013

Furlan R (2013) Build your own Google glass. IEEE Spectrum 50(1):20–21. doi:10.1109/MSPEC.2013.6395297

Laney D (2001) 3D data management: controlling data volume velocity and variety. META Group. http://blogs.gartner.com/doug-laney/files/2012/01/ad949-3D-Data-Management-Controlling-Data-Volume-Velocity-and-Variety.pdf. Accessed 7 Nov 2013

Lawler R (2013) iPhone 5s packs M7 motion-sensing chip, CoreMotion API for more accurate tracking. Engadget, Sept 2013. http://www.engadget.com/2013/09/10/iphone-5s-m7-coremotion-motion-coprocessor. Accessed 8 Nov 2013

Lisetti CL, Nasoz F (2004) Using noninvasive wearable computers to recognize human emotions from physiological signals. EURASIP J Appl Signal Process 2004:1672–1687

Llorente R, Morant M (2011) Data mining in higher education. In: Funatsu K, Hasegawa K (eds) New fundamental technologies in data mining. Intech, Croatia, pp 201–221

Looi C-K, Wong L-H, So H-J, Seow P, Toh Y, Chen W, Zhang B, Norris C (2009) Anatomy of a mobilized lesson: learning my way. Comput Educ 53(4):1120–1132

Martin T, Siewiorek DP (1994) Wearable computers. IEEE Potentials 13(3):36–38. doi:10.1109/45.310937

McClusky M (2009) The Nike experiment: How the shoe giant unleashed the power of personal metrics. Wired Magazine, June 2009. www.wired.com/medtech/health/magazine/17-07/lbnp_nike. Accessed 4 Nov 2013

Nakasugi H, Yamauchi Y (2002) Past viewer: development of wearable learning system for history education. International conference on computers in education, vol 2, pp 1311–1312, doi: 10.1109/CIE.2002.1186223

Negulescu M, Li Y (2013) Open Project: a lightweight framework for remote sharing of mobile applications. Proceedings of the 26th annual ACM symposium on user interface software and technology UIST '13, 281–290, doi: http://dx.doi.org/10.1145/2501988.2502030

Osawa N, Asai K (2006). A wearable learning support system with a head-mounted display and a foot-mounted RFID reader. International conference on information technology based higher education and training ITHET06, 523–530, doi: 10.1109/ITHET.2006.339807

Rackspace (2013) The human cloud: wearable technology from novelty to production. A social study into the impact of wearable technology. Rackspace whitepaper. www.rackspace.co.uk/humancloud. Accessed 28 Oct 2013

Santos OC, Rodriguez-Ascaso A, Boticario JG, Salmeron-Majadas S, Quirós P, Cabestrero R (2013) Challenges for inclusive affective detection in educational scenarios. Proceedings of the 7th International conference on universal access in human-computer interaction: design methods, tools, and interaction techniques for eInclusion 2013

Sharples M (2000) The design of personal mobile technologies for lifelong learning. Comput Educ 34(3–4):177–193

Soman KP, Diwakar S, Ajay V (2006) Data mining: theory and practice. PHI Learning, Delhi

Starner TE (2002) Wearable computers: no longer science fiction. IEEE Pervas Comput 1(1):86–88. doi:10.1109/MPRV.2002.993148

Thorp EO (1998) The invention of the first wearable computer. Second international symposium on wearable computers, pp 4–8, doi: 10.1109/ISWC.1998.729523

Vallurupalli S, Paydak H, Agarwal SK, Agrawal M, Assad-Kottner C (2013) Wearable technology to improve education and patient outcomes in a cardiology fellowship program—a feasibility study. Health Technol J. doi: 10.1007/s12553-013-0065-4

Yordanova K (2007). Mobile learning and integration of advanced technologies in education. International conference on computer systems and technologies—CompSysTech'07

Chapter 14
Designing Practical Activities for Skills Development

Sofia Estelles-Miguel, Gregorio Rius-Sorolla, and Mario Gil

Abstract The integration of theory and practice, together with the development of academic skills becomes an important educational objective. The case teaching method makes the participants integrate concepts and apply their proficiency to the solution of a real-life problem with the progression of their personal skills such as communication, discussion, active listening, etc. In conjunction, the numerous publications on the case-method reveal several problems when it is applied with early years undergraduate students. This paper describes our experience in adapting the case-method to teach business strategy to an earlier year undergraduate student undertaking a degree in business administration. The activity has been traced following the protocol defined for designing learning activity by the Instituto de Ciencias Educativas (ICE) of the Universidad Politécnica de Valencia (UPV).

14.1 Introduction

The actual modern definition of the case-method was first used at the Harvard Business School in 1912 (Mesny 2013) introduced by Christopher Langdell, Law Professor at the Harvard Law School (Gallego et al. 2013), having its theoretical roots in constructivism (Webb et al. 2005). It could previously be associated with the use of the case-method in education in medieval times, when it was employed

---

S. Estelles-Miguel (✉) • G. Rius-Sorolla
Departamento de Organización de Empresas, Universitat Politècnica de València,
Camino de Vera, s/n 46022, Valencia, Spain
e-mail: soesmi@omp.upv.es; greriuso@upv.es

M. Gil
C.M.Mendaur, Universidad de Navarra, Campus Universitario, s/n 31009,
Pamplona, Navarra, Spain
e-mail: mgil.4@alumni.unav.es

for solving moral or religious problems (Gallego et al. 2013) or the Socratic discourse in ancient Greece(Roy and Banerjee 2012). Today the teaching of case-method has become a very popular mode of pedagogy, especially in Business Schools, all around the world (Roy and Banerjee 2012).

Nowadays there are two highly acclaimed case-teaching styles, the Harvard case-method (HCM) and the relatively recent McAleer interactive case analysis (MICA). The original Harvard case-method is decision-focused, where the reader assumes a particular decision maker's role in a real situation, which is generally a management executive (Mesny 2013). The teacher acts as a promoter of discussions and the students have to come prepared and ready to participate actively in the class discussions. The MICA has the teacher in a secondary role, and places the student in control of the discussion (Roy and Banerjee 2012). The cases-methods can be divided into technical problem solving cases, short structured vignettes, long unstructured cases, ground-breaking cases, and anecdotes (Harling and Akridge 1998).

In general, the case-method places the student at the center of the educational process and transfers significant responsibility to the student for that which is learned (Golich 2000). It places much greater demands on the student and educator than the traditional lecture approach does. But on the other hand, it increases the level of retention compared to standard lectures (Harling and Akridge 1998). The professor becomes an orchestral director who cannot create music (learning) alone, where music will depend on each individual working together with the team as a whole (Golich 2000). The role of the professor changes from information provider to facilitator. The instructor must listen, attend to and comprehend student statements (Webb et al. 2005). The case-method helps the student to understand complex issues, to discuss politically or socially charged concerns, and to engage in informative, focused discussion (Kunselman and Johnson 2004). The case-method process can give curricular content (knowledge) and skills or competencies, such as writing, speaking, listening, information acquisition, critical thinking in a real-life environment (Golich 2000), problem identification, situation analysis, alternatives evaluation, team work and decision-making, better than the lecture method (Kester et al. 2004).

A characteristic feature of the method is that the professor has to assess in the student's process toward reaching a solution in the absence of a single correct answer. Because of this, the success of the case study method is critically dependent upon student preparation (Roy and Banerjee 2012) and the professor's knowledge of the didactic technique (Gallego et al. 2013). Therefore, the students who do not prepare the case or ignore homework will subsequently miss the related points in the seminars, behave passively in case discussions, or miss the conceptual elements in experiential exercises (Bacdayan 2004). Nowadays, due to culture changes, crisis or larger classes that makes students anonymous, or perhaps the teaching evaluation techniques related to student survey or several other potential causes, means more students with a reduced level of preparation. Therefore it is necessary to deal with the problems, with a solution like quizzing[1] (Bacdayan 2004), so herewith we will present a modification of the Harvard case-method adapted to earlier year undergraduates.

Before starting it has to be point out that the case-method has also been criticized as not being true to managerial reality, due to its inability to capture the complexity and entirety of the business environment and organizational life (Parast 2010), or not being able to work double-loop learning[2] (Argyris 1980). Also the undergraduate students, without work experience and without the basic concepts, theories, models, and analytical techniques, are not prepared to handle a case. In addition, it can be quite inefficient in terms of transmitting factual information (Kester et al. 2004). Harvard School solves the problem with the initial course by combining teaching notes before dealing with cases. It consolidates the best of both worlds, cases and lectures. In a student survey it was confirmed that in the initial courses there should be more lectures than cases, whereas in the latter courses the opposite should be true (Kester et al. 2004).

14.2 Learning Activity

14.2.1 Introduction

The activity described below is within the subject "Strategy and Organizational Design" in the Business Administration degree at the UPV. The subject is a mandatory option in their second year. It has an assignment of 6 credits (3.5 Theories and 2.5 Practices) and is given in two groups, one in English and the other in Spanish. The experiment was conducted in the English-speaking group.

The scholars conducted a series of theory sessions before the activity. This practical lesson has the purpose of reinforcing the concepts introduced in the previous lectures, with the analysis of a real case, closely related to student interest and knowledge. Most students have no work experience.

In previous years, students were accustomed to go to seminars with a quick case reading or even without any preparation, therefore attending without the required prior process of reflection for the case discussion.

For the presentation of the activity, the guidelines recommended by the ICE of the UPV (Instituto de Ciencias de la Educación 2006) for the description of an educational activity were followed. First the activity is presented, then the results obtained and finally the conclusions.

---

[1] Short, relatively frequent test on a limited amount of material.
[2] Double loop learning is when the student has to make corrections of his underlying policy or assumption in his learning process.

14.2.2 *Learning Activity Description*

14.2.2.1 Subject

The focus of the activity is "business strategy" and is based on concepts introduced in the previous theoretical lectures 1–4 (Hervas-Oliver 2013). It has the aim that students evaluate the company strategies in a real case. It also has other secondary objectives such as introducing strategic concepts that will be further deepened in the following theoretical lectures.

14.2.2.2 Moment and Number of Students

The session was held on the 11th of March (12:30–14:30)[3] in the middle of the semester. The group had 35 students.

14.2.2.3 Learning Activity Technique

The case-method technique was selected as the main line with a modification. They were encouraged to select a role from a given list with several questions, and with a personalized team studying a task of performing a short presentation.

The market segment to work on was the European football sector and the different strategy, business scopes, competitive entry barriers, etc. For the introduction of the subject it was suggested that the students find information in newspapers, on the internet or in books. Also it was recommended they read the case "Manchester United, brand of hope and glory" (Perry 2005) given in the book "Direcciones Estratégicas" (Johnson et al. 2006, 2008). The initial student presentation served as an introduction for the class case analysis and as a starting point for different discussions during the session. It gave the opportunity to explore the different key aspects of each role.

14.2.2.4 Objectives

As previously discussed, the session has a variety of goals, all of them framed in order to develop both generic and specific competences of the subject (Hervas-Oliver 2013). The competences have been set up following the requested adaptation to the degrees of European Higher Education standards (Amer-Boixareu et al. 2012) as:

(a) Specific competences:

- Analyze the environment, its key success factors, and the barriers to entry, cooperation and competition.

---

[3] In Valencia, from 1st to 19th March at 14:00, a collective recreational activity is performed in the town called the "mascletà" with large student numbers absent from classrooms.

- Analyze the corporate strategy, resources and capabilities, brand management, customer identification and actions for each segment.
- Use the various tools presented in the course (SWOT, PEST, etc.) for scenario analysis.
- Identify the culture, values, and company's strategic plan.
- Analyze the business strategy, differentiation, competitive advantage model.
- Diversification.

(b) General skills

- Instrumental skills such as analysis, synthesis, planning (5 min maximum per group), and searching for information management, written and oral communication. All in English (a second language for most participants).
- Interpersonal skills such as teamwork or international context analysis.
- Systemic skills such as research information, proposed suggestions, and steps to take by the companies.

14.2.2.5 Development

Around a month earlier it was requested that the students created groups of around six members and chose one of the proposed roles for a presentation. At the same time it was recommended that they undertook some reading for their initiation into the subject (Johnson et al. 2006, 2008) and it was requested they deepen and broaden their knowledge of the subject using the internet in order to access more recent data.

Also a rubric about a correct presentation was facilitated (Marín-Garcia 2009), so the student would have a proper view on how a presentation should be (Babiloni et al. 2010).

The roles offered were:

Type 1: Manchester United Fans

> You are a group of local fans of the Manchester United since you were born, living in the neighborhood of the Old Trafford Stadium and you have to present to the class your views on a SWOT (Strengths, Weaknesses, Opportunities y Threats) of the club today in relation to your fan club.

Type 2: Manchester United Managers

> You are a group of managers in Manchester United and you have to present your analysis on a SWOT (Strengths, Weaknesses, Opportunities y Threats) and your proposal for the future.

Type 3: Valencian Manchester United Fans

> You are a group of Manchester United fans in Valencia that have been following the club since 2 years ago, and you have to present your comparative analysis of your local team VCF-Valencia with Manchester United. (finance, projects, market strategy …)

Type 4: Manchester United investor

> You are representatives of a group of investors that have to present to your group the reasons to maintain the investment in Manchester United, or why you recommend to sell.

Type 5: Manchester United Competitors

> You are members of the board of administration of a big competitor of the Manchester United (Chelsea, Real Madrid, Barcelona …) and your president has requested your analysis of Manchester's strategy and a proposal of several actions for your club with their possible weaknesses and benefits.

Two videos were selected for the conclusion. The first one was about Real Madrid where their new resort "Real Madrid Resort Island" was presented (Ecodiario.es 2013). The video provides a different view of the usual business model that is expected from a football club, as it presents an alternative of diversification. It is a tourist park located in the UAE, with an investment of $ 1 million and it is due to open in 2015. The video is introduced to open up the idea of business alternatives in areas not previously considered by the students. The second video, as a starting point for the next session is a CNN news report from 6/2/2013 on the company Mercadona which shows continued growth despite the crisis (CNN 2013).

The student presentations were made in the order they had roles assigned. At the end of each presentation, the floor was opened for requests and questions. This time was also used to highlight the main topics and elevate open question to the class to start the discussion. On the classroom blackboard, the main concepts were brought together from each presentation along with the reflections arising from the class discussion (following the case-method technique).

After the last presentation, we reviewed all the concepts highlighted in the different presentations in order to give a complete overview. Then student teams were asked to propose an action suggestion that their company should undertake with all the information analyzed. At the end, if suggestions like the R. Madrid resort were not raised, the video was used to close the session and open up such creative ideas as an alternative to traditional lines of business.

14.2.2.6 Evaluation

For the evaluation of the session, the information presented by the team, the quality of the presentations, the clarity of their exhibitions, participation in the exhibition of all its members, and the comprehension of the contents as indicated in the rubric were all taken into account. Regarding the case-method, the evaluation was based upon participation, level of arguments (Harling and Akridge 1998), and active listening (Golich 2000). The session has 0.25 out of 10 of the final grade of the course.

In another online session, designed to ensuring that the concepts had been learned, each student was asked at the end of the session to highlight a concept that had impacted them most.

14.2.2.7 Times

The class lasted 2 h with exposures of 5–7 min, plus 5–10 min to highlight important elements of each presentation, writing them on the board and undertaking class discussions. The remaining 10 min were used for the video presentation. The session requires previous individual work and teamwork of 2–3 h for researching information, joint review, and presentation.

14.2.2.8 Material

We used a projector, whiteboard, audio, and a computer with wireless mouse for presentations.

14.2.2.9 Observations

Students are often motivated to find information on this topic, football. On the other hand, the fact of having to explain it in front of their peers gives the necessary pressure to work hard on it. A priori, it was argued that students used to attend the lessons without having read the cases, but with this methodology for the case-method we can see self-motivation before the session, allowing a successful development of a strategic analysis of the company, industry, brand development, etc.

14.2.2.10 Recommendations

At the beginning of the session it is decisive to reinforce active listening and to follow the defined times for each presentation, in order to have enough time for the discussions. Also, it is important to remember that the objective is to take decisions and actions supported with the tools learned. And it is interesting to highlight the main participation points at the end of each presentation.

14.3 Results

The session was very fruitful. The students were identified with different roles and copious information was provided (internet, accounting, newspaper, etc.). To the extent, the original case (Perry 2005) was quickly treated and new problems were analyzed with well worked solutions.

Also, as the interventions were short and the discussions were animated over the different conclusions, the session was rich with interesting discussions. A last review of all the main points of the session was done in order to give a general view of the concepts learned, so the students left with a feeling of a great effort done, completing the feedback cycle (Golich 2000).

After the session, students were asked to rate the lesson and if they would recommend it to a friend (anonymously). The overwhelming response was "yes" with a rating of 3.86 out of 5 (5 being the most positive). One thing that was appreciated highly was the concept of teamwork, where each group member is responsible for his learning as well as the other members of the group (Goméz-González et al. 2012).

14.4 Conclusions

When working on a subject close to the students (football teams), the interest in interest is easily achieved, a basic requirement in order to maximize their direct involvement in their own learning process (Bain 2011). Also the students gain confidence as they can solve or identify the problems with the newly introduced analysis tools. And finally, the challenge of making a public presentation adds greater concentration and interest, a equivalent pressure of quizzing (Bacdayan 2004), in doing their homework.

The case was also done in the Spanish group, but following the pure Harvard methodology for the case-method as reading, preparing several questions at home and getting to class ready for the discussion on the professor's open questions. It was found that the main body of the students arrived at the session without having read the material, without investigating the information available on the internet, so the group had to be given 20 min of the session to let them read it.

Instead, the English group had undertaken previous study, with the class-based activity, internalized concepts and even changed underlying assumptions or personal goals (double-loop learning). Also, the students were able to answer questions such as "what are they for? Once I have it what can I do?" regarding tools previously introduced in the theoretical sessions, such as SWOT.

The lesson was done with the assistance of all the students enrolled despite the "mascletà."

References

Amer-Boixareu MA, Bernadàs-Tel S, Moreno-Vendrell A (2012) Proyecto integrado: una alternativa metodológica para las asignaturas de tipo teórico. In: XX Congreso Universitario de Innovación Educativa en las Enseñanzas Técnicas CUIEET XX Las Palmas de Gran Canaria

Argyris C (1980) Some limitations of the case method: experiences in a management development program. Acad Manage Rev 5:291–298

Babiloni E, Guijarro E, Rodríguez I, Estellés S (2010) Las matrices de valoración como herramienta de evaluación formativa: aplicación a una presentación oral. In: XVIII Congreso Universitario de Innovación Educativa en las Enseñanzas Técnicas Santander

Bacdayan P (2004) Comparison of management faculty perspectives on quizzing and its alternatives. J Educ Bus 80:5–9

Bain K (2011) What the best college teachers do. Harvard University Press, Harvard
CNN (2013) Spanish retailer bucks trend. http://www.youtube.com/watch?v=tuIT0ujvhX4 Accessed 11 Jan 2013
Ecodiario.es (2013) Real Madrid Resort Island, el sueño de Florentino Pérez se hace realidad. http://www.youtube.com/watch?v=ZOY_HISHAf4. Accessed 11 Jan 2013
Gallego A, Fortunato MS, Rossi SL, Korol SE, Moretton JA (2013) Case method in the teaching of food safety. J Food Sci Educ 12:42–47
Golich VL (2000) The ABCs of case teaching. Int Stud Perspect 1:11–29
Goméz-González JF, Díaz B, Fabiani-Bendicho P (2012) Evaluación cooperativa frente a la evaluación objetiva mediante prueba individual en la enseñanza práctica en la ingeniería. In: XX Congreso Universitario de Innovación Educativa en las Enseñanzas Técnicas CUIEET XX Las Palmas de Gran Canaria
Harling KF, Akridge J (1998) Using the case method of teaching. Agribusiness 14:1–14
Hervas-Oliver J (2013) Guía docente "Estrategia y Diseño de la Organización". http://www.upv.es/pls/oalu/sic_asi.Busca_Asi?p_codi=11747&p_caca=2012&P_IDIOMA=c&p_vista=%282013%29. Accessed 11 Jan 2013
Instituto de Ciencias de la Educación (2006). Plan de Acciones para la Convergencia Europea (PACE) Guía docente de la UPV: criterios para su elaboración. http://www.upv.es/vece/central_pace.htm. Accessed 11 Jan 2013
Johnson G, Scholes K, Whittington R (2006) Dirección estratégica. Prentice-Hall, Madrid
Johnson G, Scholes K, Whittington R (2008) Exploring corporate strategy: text and cases. Pearson Education, Harlow
Kester GW, Hoover SA, McGoun EG (2004) Cases versus lectures: undergraduate student perspectives. In: Financial education association 2004 annual meeting, Orlando
Kunselman JC, Johnson KA (2004) Using the case method to facilitate learning. Coll Teach 52:87–92
Marín-Garcia JA (2009) Los Alumnos y los profesores como Evaluadores. Aplicación a la calificación de las presentaciones orales. Rev Españ de Pedag 67:79–97
Mesny A (2013) Taking stock of the century-long utilization of the case method in management education. Can J Admin Sci 30:56–66
Parast MM (2010) Effectiveness of case study in enhancing student learning in operations management. Oper Supply Chain Manage 3:49–58
Perry B (2005) Manchester United: brand of hope and glory. University of Wolverhampton Business School, Wolverhampton
Roy S, Banerjee P (2012) Understanding students experience of transition from lecture mode to case-based teaching in a management school in India. J Educ Change 13:487–509
Webb HW, Gill G, Poe G (2005) Teaching with the case method online: pure versus hybrid approaches. Dec Sci J Innov Educ 3:223–250

Index

A
Active learning, 110, 112
Active methodologies, 77, 84, 110–113, 115
Adaptive learning, 2
Adult students, 118, 120–123
Appreciative inquiry, 104
Aronson puzzle, 111
Assessment, 6, 13–17, 19, 20, 23–29, 44, 48, 65, 66, 68, 76–84, 88, 89, 91, 92, 96, 100, 102
Augmented learning, 1–9
Autonomous learning, 77, 80
Average students, 76, 77, 84

B
Big data, 127–135
Blended learning, 23–28
Bologna Declaration, 53, 54, 58
Bologna process, 53–54, 75–84
Business, 8, 19, 20, 26, 41–48, 78, 79, 89, 92, 103, 104, 106, 119, 120, 139–144
  decision-making, 46
  schools, 139, 140
  strategy, 142, 143
Business Models, 106, 144

C
Cluster analysis, 62, 63, 69, 70
Cmaptools, 46
cMOOCs. *See* Connective MOOC (cMOOCs)
Co-creation innovation, 117–124

Collaborative learning, 3, 84, 109, 113
Collaborative methodologies, 77
Collaborative work, 3, 77, 83, 84
Companies, 2, 7, 8, 68, 70, 88, 89, 91, 92, 95, 102–104, 109–115, 119, 120, 123, 124, 128, 130, 131, 142–145
Competence assessment, 14, 16, 24, 26, 78, 79, 83, 87–96
Competency(ies), 14, 16, 20, 24, 26–28, 31–38, 42–44, 54, 76–84, 87–96, 105, 109–115, 124, 140, 142
Competitive advantage, 123, 143
Concept mapping, 41–48, 61–72
Conceptual aptitudes, 48
Condensed classroom, 3, 7, 8
Connected/collaborative learning, 2, 3, 84, 109, 113
Connecting ideas, 105
Connective MOOC (cMOOCs), 13, 20
Continuous assessment grade, 80–84
Cooperative learning, 110
Creative tension, 92–94
Critical thinking, 140
Curricula development, 53
Customer orientation, 123

D
Data processing, 134, 135
Decision maker's role, 140
Decision making process, 45, 122, 123
Delphi survey, 120
Differentiation strategy, 123
Digital platform, 88, 89

E

Education, 2, 3, 5–9, 12, 16, 18–20, 23–29, 31–38, 41–43, 45, 51–59, 61–72, 76, 88, 99–106, 109, 110, 118, 119, 121, 127–135, 139, 142
Educational innovation, 112
Educational institutions, 8, 12–17, 19, 20, 118
Educational market, 119, 120, 122, 123
EHEA. *See* European Higher Education Area (EHEA)
Employer, 118, 120–123
EQF. *See* European Qualifications Framework (EQF)
Ethical competence, 32, 34
Ethical learning, 32
Ethics, 32, 33, 37, 38
European Higher Education Area (EHEA), 32, 41, 42, 53, 76, 78, 84, 88
European Qualifications Framework (EQF), 32
Evaluation, 28, 36–38, 56, 58, 59, 88, 90–95, 110, 111, 113, 114, 133, 134, 140, 144
Evaluation instruments, 113
Exam correction, 133
Exam grade, 80–83
Excellent students, 76, 77, 83, 84
External experts, 104

F

Facilitation, 24, 33, 44, 46, 65, 68, 77, 84, 102–105, 123, 140, 143
Faculty framework, 123
Feedback, 12, 14, 15, 29, 77, 89, 103, 121, 146
Final grade, 25, 76, 80–84, 144
Financial Accounting, 26, 27
Flipped Classroom, 1–9
Flip teaching, 7
Formative assessment, 23–29
Free education, 16

G

Generic skills, 42
Google Glass, 129–132, 134, 135
Group dynamics, 62, 65, 113

H

Higher education, 12, 23–29, 31–38, 41, 45, 51–59, 61–72, 76, 88, 109, 118, 119, 121, 127–135, 142

Higher education institutions, 12, 25, 52
Hybrid Classroom, 3

I

Industrial Technologies Engineering degree course, 46
Innovation, 20, 24, 25, 29, 32, 33, 42, 51–59, 64, 72, 88, 92, 103, 104, 109, 112, 117–124
Innovation in pedagogy, 29, 51–59
Instrumental competencies, 80, 81, 83, 84
Instrumental skills, 143
Intellectual competence, 32, 33
Interpersonal competencies, 81, 83
Interpersonal skills, 77, 83, 143

K

Key points, 72, 123
Khan Academy, 1–9, 18, 19
Knowledge, 2, 5, 6, 11–14, 18–20, 24, 26, 27, 32–35, 37, 42, 43, 45–48, 53–55, 59, 63, 76–78, 80, 83, 84, 88, 90, 92, 100–106, 110–112, 119, 123, 127–135, 140, 141, 143
  building, 127–135
  management, 63, 100–103
  mapping, 43, 45, 48

L

Learning, 1–9, 12–20, 23–29, 32–38, 41–48, 53–55, 57–59, 76–78, 80, 82–84, 88–90, 96, 100–106, 109–115, 119, 127–129, 131–134, 140–146
  activity, 25, 37, 38, 141–145
  design, 16, 26–28, 35, 42, 144
  experiences, 13, 25, 36, 42, 57–59, 127
  feedback, 77
  organization, 100–103
  process, 7, 13, 20, 24–26, 28, 33–36, 38, 42, 44, 59, 76–78, 80, 89, 96, 100, 102, 103, 105, 106, 110, 111, 127, 133, 141, 146
  strategy, 41–48, 112
Least squeres ordinaries (OLS), 81
Lego Serious Play (LSP), 99–106

M

Massive Open Online Courses (MOOCs), 1–9, 11–20

Master degree, 53
Masters, 5, 45, 53, 64, 68, 72, 88, 89, 91–95, 114, 117–124
Members, 15, 18, 19, 32, 46, 63, 77, 83, 84, 101–103, 111, 120–122, 143–146
Metaphors, 101, 105
Methodological renovation, 109
Methodology, 14, 26–28, 35, 42–47, 55–59, 62, 64, 72, 77, 79, 84, 88, 91–92, 104, 109–115, 120–122, 145, 146
Model postgraduate institutions, 118, 119, 123, 124
MOOCs. *See* Massive Open Online Courses (MOOCs)
Moodle, 26, 28
Moral competence, 31–38
Morality, 32
Moral knowledge, 32, 37
Moral learning, 34

N
New classroom technologies, 131–132
New technologies for education, 8, 52

O
Online learning, 6, 7
Open access, 12, 18
Open education, 12
Organizational changes, 5
Organization development, 104

P
Pedagogical development, 55
Pedagogical innovation, 29, 51–59
Pedagogical models, 53, 55, 58
Pedagogical strategies, 55, 59
Peer learning, 105
Personal competencies, 81, 83, 94–96
Postgraduate, 87–96, 118–120, 123, 124
Post-Lecture Classroom, 3, 8
Principles of Business Organisation course, 42, 43, 46–48
Prior knowledge, 43, 105
Proactive market orientation, 119, 123
Problem solving, 5, 6, 102, 134, 140
Professional performance, 52, 76

Q
Qualitative assessment, 48

R
Role playing, 35

S
Scaffolding, 28
Self-assessment by students, 78, 79
Skills, 3, 5, 6, 14, 20, 24, 32, 34, 36, 42, 53, 76–78, 83, 84, 88–90, 92, 95, 100–104, 110–112, 124, 139–146
Skills development, 110, 139–146
Smartphone, 4, 128–132
Smartwatch, 128–132, 134, 135
Social competencies, 88
Soft skills, 3
Spanish universities, 42, 76, 88
Specific competence, 34, 42, 43, 142
Story telling, 105
Strategy, 13–14, 19, 20, 24, 27, 34, 37, 41–48, 52, 53, 55, 59, 89, 95, 103, 104, 111, 112, 118, 119, 123, 128, 141–144
Students, 5–7, 12–20, 24–29, 32, 34–38, 42–48, 52–59, 63–65, 68, 70–72, 75–84, 87–96, 99, 100, 105, 106, 109–115, 118–123, 131–135, 140–146
  autonomy, 57
  behaviour, 82
  characterization, 58
  empowerment, 59
  interaction, 70
  performance, 75–84
Systemic competences, 80, 81, 83, 84
Systems models, 106

T
Teachers' perception, 51–59
Teachers' profile, 52
Teaching–learning processes, 24–26, 28, 42, 59, 76, 78, 84, 89, 96
Teaching Machine, 2
Teaching services, 71, 72
Teamwork, 33, 35, 109–115, 143, 145, 146
Technical competence, 38
Technical learning, 34, 35
Thinkertoys, 103
Thinking with topic at hand, 62

Tools, 2–5, 7, 8, 15, 25, 26, 28, 29, 35, 42–48, 62, 63, 72, 87–96, 102, 103, 111, 112, 120, 143, 145, 146

U
Universities, 2, 6–8, 12, 13, 18, 19, 23–26, 32–34, 36, 38, 41, 42, 46, 57, 64, 65, 68, 72, 76, 78, 88, 89, 91, 92, 95, 96, 103, 115, 117–124, 129, 130
University education, 42
University staff, 123

V
Value Proposition, 12–14, 19
Virtues, 32, 33, 35–38, 62, 83
Visual understanding environment, 46

W
Wearable computers, 127–135
WebQuest, 27, 28